Rev. Fred Sterling ...surprise
me, therefore, that *Gui...* ...onal yet
of the published Kirael ...The insights are
profound, but the real message is human enablement.

—**Lee Carroll**, Author of the *Kryon* channeled series, and co-author of
The Indigo Children series of best selling books.

Guide to the Unseen Self is as much for the student of metaphysics as it is
for those making their first inquiry into why life is the way it is. The wisdom
of Kirael comes through the answers to many questions that we all ask about
our lives and the world in which we live. The keys to purpose, desire, surrender
and allowance lie in these pages.

—**Roger Miles**, Publisher, *Elohim Journal*

Kirael and Reverend Sterling have gifted us with a grand opportunity to
grow and understand our spirituality. This volume had a "blossoming" effect
on my spiritual journey, each chapter an unfolding of an inner awareness of
the Ten Principles of Conscious Creation.

—**Barbara Miyashiro**, Teacher and Healer

Guide to the Unseen Self is a lovely journey through our many stages of
Life. Kirael teaches us how closely we are all connected to each other. I highly
recommend this marvelous book and look upon it as a wondrous and much
needed addition to the field of human consciousness.

—**Sheldan Nidle**, founder of the Planetary Activation Organization and
author of *You Are Becoming a Galactic Human, Your First Contact* and *Selamat Ja!*

I feel we are truly blessed to be gifted with the wisdom, wit and
compassion of Kirael. The information he brings forth is cutting-edge and
not just a rehash of old concepts. Kirael may not always say what we want to
hear, but he does tell us what we need to know. The guidelines and insights
he gives in his messages are indispensable during these times of great change.

—**Ronna Herman**, author of *On Wings of Light, The Golden Promise*,
and the metafiction trilogy, *Once Upon a New World*

Other Books by Fred Sterling

Kirael: The Great Shift
Kirael Volume II: The Genesis Matrix

For Tapes of Live Kirael Sessions Contact:

Honolulu Church of Light
1539 Kapiolani Blvd.
Honolulu, Hawaii 96814
Phone: 1-800-390-1886
        (808) 952-0880
Fax: (808) 952-0660
Web Site: www.Kirael.com

The Kirael Collection

GUIDE TO THE
UNSEEN SELF

To Nancy
Mahalo

FRED STERLING

Lightways
Publishing

IX1093

GUIDE TO THE UNSEEN SELF

Published in 2002
Copyright © 2002 by Fred Sterling
All rights reserved.

The Publishing Company for the Great Shift in Consciousness

LIGHTWAYS PUBLISHING
P.O. Box 27648
Honolulu, HI 96827 USA

Phone (808) 945-3965
Orders 1-800-390-1886
(808) 952-0880
Fax (808) 952-0660
Web site www.kirael.com/lightways

Cover Art: Lance Agena
Author Photo: Gene Tamashiro

Printed in the United States of America

ISBN 0-9675353-9-5

Sterling, Fred, 1946-
    Guide to the unseen self / Fred Sterling.
    p. cm. -- (The Kirael collection)
    LCCN 2002109570
    ISBN 0-9675353-9-5

    1. Reality. 2. Ontology. 3. Spirituality.
    4. Self-Realization--Religious aspects.   I. Title.

BD331.S84 2002   110
                    QBI33-631

ACKNOWLEDGMENTS

Behold the untiring group of individuals who have made this work possible. Although the names are many, each person is honored in my heart for bringing the words of Master Kirael to their highest light.

The names are in alphabetical order for it would be impossible to place them in order of importance. Each person has chosen to move to new levels of growth by being a part of this undertaking, and in that each has a part of my heart. I recognize each person whose name is on this page as my sister and my brother. Our oneness shines in this book. Together, may we aid in the healing of the world.

My first words of gratitude go to the transcribers of the "Kirael Shift Report" sessions and the "Evenings with Kirael": Sonja Langley, Barbara Miyashiro and Rose Taylor.

My heartfelt thanks to the editors who brought clarity to the transcribed materials: Lori Domingo, Karen Eakman, Jerry Fujioka, Sonja Langley, Rev. Carol Morishige, Karen Nielsen, Patti Sterling and Karen Yue.

My gratitude to the special focus group participants: Lori Domingo, Karen Eakman, Jerry Fujioka, Diana George, Sonja Langley, Phillip Lau, Rev. Carol Morishige, Rev. Melvin Morishige, Karen Nielsen, Patti Sterling, Karen Yue, and our sound technician, Rick Sterling.

Much appreciation to all the dedicated proofreaders of edited chapters: Julie Bower, Elmy Brown, Lori Domingo, Karen Eakman, Jerry Fujioka, Diana George, Tom Holowach, Gail Jan Kaneshiro, Sonja Langley, Jean Marutani, Rev. Melvin Morishige, Karen Nielsen, Frances Shomura, Patti Sterling, Elizabeth Weatherford and Karen Yue. A special thanks also to Barbara Miyashiro for proofreading the final manuscript.

To the creative team, Sarah Melissa Pollack and Stacie T. Lau for the original book cover art and concept; Lance Agena for cover art; and Lance and Kehau Agena, for the book formatting and design, a big thank you.

To the marketing focus group: David Bower, Lori Domingo, Jerry Fujioka, Karen Nielsen, Rev. Melvin Morishige, Robert Rotondi, Kan Shimada, and Patti Sterling, for your passion and clarity, I am forever grateful.

Were it not for the loving guidance of Master Kirael, Master Jesus, Angel Teeny, the Lightways Council of Angels, the 144 Grand Masters and the 188 Angels guiding everyone working on the project, this book would not be. You are honored in the Creator's Light.

And finally, all who attended the "Evenings with Kirael" and "Kirael

Shift Report" channeling sessions deserve special recognition. Your questions of Master Kirael have made all of this possible.

Many of you who read these words may have the privilege of knowing the people named on these pages. I invite you, and all the readers, to place your hand on this page and wish all who are listed here well.

Aloha and mahalo,

Rev. Fred Sterling

A SPECIAL THANK YOU TO THE DONALD KIESS FAMILY

To Don, the father, who heals with deeds of passion
To Daughter, Kitty, who found her strength in healing others and healed herself
To Daughter, Kristy, a dear heart teacher who let all find their courage to heal
To Son-in-law Eero, the giant who heals with the softest touch

Because of this family, I find strength

"The Rev."

CONTENTS

Chapter 3
THE BLUEPRINT OF LIFE:
YOUR FIRST SEVEN YEARS

Chapter 4
HEALING KARMA

Chapter 9

9-11: A Wake-Up Call for Lightworkers

To all who find the path of knowing,
Life can be just as you desire.
In your courage to shape life to your dreams,
We collectively find a better existence.

—Rev. Fred Sterling

PUBLISHER'S PREFACE

This book is for all seekers of truth. It comes at a time when the world has seen upheaval at the close of one millennium and the dawn of a new one. Such times often herald new beginnings, marked by the emergence of new energy and new thought.

Some may argue that nothing is new, only recycled and repackaged with a new twist. Some say many books on spirituality seem to essentially say the same thing. So what sets this book of channeled material apart from the rest? The title, *Guide to the Unseen Self*, offers clues in answer to that question.

It has been said, "When the student is ready, the teacher shall appear." In this case, the teacher comes forth as a presence of light to guide those seeking to make sense of their lives. A light being of a dimension known as the Guidance Realm, Kirael has no physical presence other than that of his medium, Rev. Fred Sterling. For over ten years, Kirael and Rev. Sterling have been in this unique partnership, meeting with people who seek truth at levels beyond what is easily accessible in our human world.

Kirael has said, "Knowledge is in the eye of the beholder." Indeed, this is a time for seeing a whole new world of possibilities, and Kirael offers to guide any who seeks to enter within. Many who know Kirael have learned of him through friends, books, magazines, and recordings of public or private channeling sessions. All have been guided to him when they, as students, were ready. Today, an awakening is taking place within each person alive on the planet today. The students are ready; the teacher is here.

This book, *Guide to the Unseen Self*, is a collection of live channeling sessions with Kirael. Following these monthly "Evenings with Kirael" or "Kirael Shift Report" sessions, many have said, "That session was so beautiful! More people should know about Kirael and Rev. Sterling!" Indeed, it is time for spiritual seekers throughout the world to experience what the people in Hawaii have enjoyed thus far.

You will find that in each channeling session, Kirael's intensity will vary. In some, his mood and tone reflect the events of the world at the time. Entering the new millennium and the September 11, 2001 terrorist attacks are examples of such. At other times you will find Kirael more relaxed, as evidenced by his lapses into a slight Scottish accent, and his use of phrases such as "a wee bit" or "me medium." In every instance, however, you will find him impassioned and focused, answering every question posed to him in the fullness of love and truth.

Much of the material for this book was recorded in 2000 and 2001. The topics reflect the acceleration of spiritual and planetary motions towards healing and evolution as Earth enters a period of transition, otherwise known as the Shift.

The transcripts of these sessions have been edited with the intent of offering Kirael's words of wisdom in the greatest clarity in written form. Kirael often creates new words when he finds the human language limiting for the information he reveals. Hence, you will find Kirael's new words and phrases throughout. Additional phrases have been also been added during the editing process—with much prayer for assistance and guidance from Kirael and other unseen guides and angels—to make the beauty of these messages clear on the written page. Questions and answers of a more personal note from the sessions have remained just that, personal.

Within these pages, Kirael invites you to enter into a Great Room of Discovery. He encourages you to indulge in every possibility of truth about the unseen parts of you. And if you don't "get it" after reading a passage the first time, don't be disheartened. Kirael has said that his words are always embedded with seven layers of understanding.

There is but one request: Hold off any judgment until you have read the entire book. To you, the readers, Kirael says, "When you have read this book entirely without judgment, only then shall you awaken to the fullness of *your* journey. *The Great Room is the truth of who you are.*"

And if all else fails, do as many of us have already done on occasion: say "Kirael" three times and he will be with you.

We are honored to bring forth the words of Kirael and Rev. Fred Sterling, and to collaborate with them—in prayer, meditation, sleepstate programming, and masterminding, the tools of Conscious Creation.

The Publishers

INTRODUCTION

The Medium

How does one awaken into a world so intriguing and filled with realities never before seen and then pretend that it was not real? Or pretend not to remember every detail of that world when you can? Or remember worlds that hold deeper truths of existence than you could ever experience in the dreamstate that is our human awareness?

Is there something encoded deep within a person that makes a person a medium? I look back on my life and know that being a medium is the only true path I could have chosen. I had a burning desire to share with the rest of the world what I was experiencing. I knew that would brand me as different, but it was all right, because I *was* different. I had crossed the barriers of self-imposed illusion that we use to believe that we are all alone out there. I had found a way to be a conduit for information that could be shared between many dimensional realities.

What is a medium if not one who literally stands between two powerful sources of light? The first and most easily recognized source of light is the material, or human plane. The second source of light is a place far beyond human comprehension that stretches the mind to inconceivable levels of awareness and leaves the traveler literally wondering just how far one can go.

I now know that a medium is one whom the world of guidance views as a conduit between the worlds. The beautiful light beings of the Guidance Realm know levels of truth that we in the human world can only dream of. And to fulfill their Creator-ordained tasks of working with realities in varying stages of evolution, they must seek out those who have the ability to, shall we say, walk between the worlds.

Was I called to this task? If I was, it must have come from something that happened thousands of years ago. So many parts of my journey blend together, yet I now see that my choices were not as many as I earlier believed. Ultimately, it was not so difficult to walk away from a twenty-year career and begin a new life as a healer, spiritual teacher and medium for Kirael, a seventh-dimensional light being of the Guidance Realm.

And So It Continues

Being asked by the world of spirit to bring forth messages that are helping to change the world as we know it is a humbling experience. I am honored to collaborate with Kirael and other unseen forces of light as another of Kirael's books takes form. I also share, along with you the readers, many of your questions. In a sense, I watch Kirael's work unfold just as you the reader do.

Two books ago, we were given a guidebook to the great shift in consciousness in *Kirael: The Great Shift*. Then we were taken on a guided journey of the origins of the Earth matrix in the second book, *Kirael Volume II: The Genesis Matrix*.

And now we have the book, *Guide to the Unseen Self*. In the initial stages of this book project, I knew the beauty of Kirael's words would have to be as clear to the reader who meets Kirael for the first time on these pages as to the person who hears him in a live session. The beauty and passion with which Kirael communicates and his uncanny ability to see everything in a positive light had to be maintained.

Then, when I had the opportunity to read the first few pages of this manuscript, I immediately felt the fullness of Master Kirael's energy and knew that everything was in total perfection. I was truly "hearing" Kirael in his most enlightening form. His loving energy filled every page and I found myself following his every word. What else could be expected from a true master?

The Kirael Collection is a new compilation of channeled Kirael Sessions assembled by subject matter into a series of nine books. In this first book, *Guide to the Unseen Self,* you will find some of the most interesting interviews we have had with Kirael. More importantly, you will discover in these pages why you are on the Earth plane in one of the most exciting periods of the Creator's evolution.

The more we learn, the more we discover how much more there is to learn. Enlightenment is never-ending, my friends. So let's take this journey together with Kirael, and if you are like me, when you reach the final page, you will only be thirsting for more.

It's a time of great awareness, my friends. *It's the Great Shift.*

Rev. Fred Sterling

GUIDE TO THE
UNSEEN SELF

1 *You Are A Lightworker*

Opening Statement

KIRAEL: Good evening.

The mission that each of you has chosen is to awaken the world to the Light Reality of which everything is made. This is not the easiest task that you will take on in any lifetime, yet each of you has made your commitments, and now we will see how it unfolds.

Everybody uses the words, I want to be enlightened. To begin with, I think you should change the spelling to *i-n*-lightened and then you become *en*-lightened. You start by placing the light at the very core of your soul and by becoming aware of the beauty of the wondrous light that exists within every part of your being. In that way, you activate the Light Source within you.

Let's start this evening with a short exercise. First, allow light to enter your crown chakra and see it penetrating the very core of your anatomy. See the light begin to glow. As it becomes stronger, feel it in each and every cell of your body. As the light expands out through the skin, you will find yourself in a wee ball of light. Now, everyone here in this gathering, expand your light just a wee bit more. While you do that, I will work with my medium [Rev. Fred Sterling] until each of your lights amasses as a whole. Then, I will add my own light to yours. Together, let us energize what we are now. Feel the light surround us, feel it as it permeates within us. You have just become "en-lightened."

How do you feel now? Wasn't that beautiful?

What is a Lightworker?

You may ask, what is a Lightworker? I suggest to you that a Lightworker is an energy pattern that has awakened to the potential of his or her "lightbeing-ness." It is a person who is awakening to the inner charge of his or her core essence. Simply put, Lightworkers are those who choose to live on different levels of awareness, which set them apart from the masses. They have recognized their core light is one and the same with the very core of Creation.

In their own awakening process, Lightworkers are becoming enlightened. They know that there is no separation from their Creator Essence. They clearly understand that they can speak with all forms of guidance, all levels of awareness. They recognize that they no longer need to base their lives on fear as they have learned that much of recorded human history was a fear-driven process.

The beauty is that Lightworkers are now awakening to the realization that Love is the answer to every part of their reality. They are able to see Love as a single energy force, with no duality force to oppose it. Humans have been taught that the other side of love is hate or fear, when in truth, there is no opposite. How can there be an opposing force to the force of love when Love is simply the emanation of light from the core essence of the Creator?

At this time all around the world, you the Lightworkers are amassing in love. And like the ripples from a pebble tossed in a brook, you are emanating the energy of light to the rest of the world. There are some Lightworkers who would prefer to remain as "closet" Lightworkers. They are the Lightworkers in powerful positions who are not yet ready to stand up and admit their true identity. Each time they have shown their potential for love, the darkened energy forces surrounding them have misconstrued their love as weakness. Indeed, many have been brainwashed into thinking that fear is power, and love is weakness. Yet the truth remains: each of you holds a spark of the Creator's Light within you, and each of you knows how to make love work here on the Earth plane.

"Why can't we speak from love?" you ask. To speak from love means you would have to express yourself from your core essence. That is not easy for most humans to do. Most humans think that speaking from love would keep them from using all the things they have learned in this lifetime about love. They fear losing all those things that slip and slide away from the essence of love. Lightworkers can speak from love, but first they need to always, always search their inner core before speaking. I cannot say this enough. When Lightworkers speak, let it always be from their heart essence, the core of their value light—that Light which is the Creator Itself.

Let's look at Lightworkers from even another perspective. Whether anyone would like to admit it, every single human being on the face of this planet is a Lightworker. Every single one is born of the God Light, which makes each of you a light being in "sound personification." That means, to become human, you have allowed your light particles to be so closely amassed together that you appear to be of a solid form. Yet what appears as solid is but an illusion created from light and sound for the purpose of the human journey. In other words, in order to experience conquests within the journey (and I didn't use "conquests" by accident), you have had to make your illusion fit the journey. And because each journey is in a constant state of evolution, each person has chosen specific levels of evolution to awaken to, and thereby to see through the illusion. Thus, every human being is a Lightworker. The only question is what degree they are willing to let the light illuminate within and through them.

Yes, but what about the so-called "dangerous" people of society? Are they Lightworkers? In truth, they are younger souls. The difference is that their inner light has become so densely amassed that they have literally become a shaded or darkened energy. It is not that they are not of the Light. It only means they have pulled in their light so tightly that they do not feel the Light. So, when you encounter such a person, even those who would call you "airy fairy," just try to understand and not become upset. Just be clear that their own beauty of light is so compressed within them that they are unable to see your light.

"Lightworkers amassing" should probably be rephrased as "Lightworkers awakening." This might make more sense, given the fact that every single person on the Earth plane is a Lightworker. And now it is a matter of the Lightworkers bringing their energy to a higher vibration so that more people experience what this light is about. It is not about going out and joining the Lightworkers force. You are already a part of the light force. Your life force, that unseen part of you is already amassed in light.

You have heard me say many times that being a Lightworker is not about running around and shouting from the rooftops about how beautiful your light is. It is about *being* the light. It is about doing the physical, human journey with your light lit brightly. With the physical body that you have chosen for this journey, I now ask that you bring forth your core light and expand it outward. When you bring "in" your force, the denser the particles become and the darker it seems to appear. The more you release your light "out" from your energy field, the more your light expands.

The Collective Energy of Grass Lawns: A Metaphor

Let's look for a moment at grass. You have grass here on the Earth plane. And you have buzzing machines that go across the grass to cut it down. The minute the lawn mower engine starts up, every blade of grass within that area is immediately aware of what is about to take place. Whether the plot of grass is five feet or five acres makes no difference. And just like you, the grass is made up of energy. So when the first blades of grass sense that they are about to be cut down, they issue a command for all grass to promptly begin a new phase of growth. In this way, the grass avoids going into a state of fear. Then, by the time the mower is busy moving across the lawn, the grass has already entered into a new phase of growth.

Grass grows fast in the beginning. Then the growth phase slows down, until the mower comes by again. During the slowdown phase, the grass focuses on fulfilling its evolutionary task on this planet, which is to oxygenate Mother Earth and her inhabitants. That is its job, and it knows how to do it. You might think the grass dies in fear or goes into panic when it sees the mower coming, but it doesn't. It simply sends out its energy in the form of light, letting the rest of the grass know what is about to happen. From there, everything moves into action.

Relate that now to the Lightworkers. Lightworkers are trying to emanate light out into the world. They are trying their very best, but the truth is that there are many more grass mowers than there are Lightworkers right now. And because Lightworkers are nonviolent—at least we would like to pray that is the case—they are willing to sometimes stand in front of the mower and be mowed over. When one Lightworker sends out a call to other Lightworkers, all of the Lightworkers receive the call. They know when the mower is out. They also know what to do. As with the grass, Lightworkers automatically go within and bring their light to a vibrant space. Then they direct it wherever it is needed. The energy that is sent forth is Truth.

Unfortunately, some enlightened people are in self-imposed solitary realities which make it difficult for them to remain connected with the other Lightworkers. Hence, they are not vibrating at a level that can hear the command to raise their light vibrations. This leaves them feeling vulnerable and alone when the mowers come. My point is that the Lightworker force is not yet at sufficient numbers to guarantee that all Lightworkers receive the SOS to collectively activate their light energies.

All Lightworkers, please listen. If the mower is going to push on you, you have to pop yourself back up, and grow even bigger and greener, and generate more oxygen and more light into the Earth plane. I think they call that a metaphor. As the human light begins to recognize more of its God presence, more of its Creator presence, the Lightworkers will have more of a powerful strength together. They still will be mowed down, so to speak, but hopefully not in a forceful manner. The truth of the Lightworker energy calls for a brand new way of thinking, and we all know that a brand new way of thinking is not something the human world accepts very easily.

A Lightworker is not someone who wakes up one day and says, "I am a Lightworker!" It is someone who wakes up one day and says, "Oh, my God, what is happening to me? Why is it that I see the world differently today? I don't want to do it. I don't want to do it." And they run and hide again and again. The Lightworkers are hiding, my friends, because it is frightening out there. Why is that? It is because part of being a Lightworker is taking responsibility for your own inner love and inner awakening. A lot of people don't want to do that right away. So as they begin to awaken, they run and hide under the covers. Eventually though, there will be enough Lightworkers emitting beautiful light around the world. Like the grass, the trees, the frogs, single-cell amoeba, all is made of light.

Everything is Light; therefore, everything is connected. You are all personifications of the Light, and you are all connected. In the illusion of time and space, you might think you are creating a space between you and others. In truth, however, while you are sitting in one part of the room and my medium is sitting facing you, your energy is one with my medium. Likewise, if you become aggravated or happy—either one—those around you will be affected. As I said before, everything is connected, so the more Lightworkers think about understanding love and moving their lives into brighter spaces, the more other people will awaken to their own light. The challenge is not about creating a force of Lightworkers. It is about keeping your light so bright that the Lightworkers become aware of themselves as Lightworkers.

Shall we now open to your questions?

Questions & Answers

Why Lightworkers are Amassing

Good evening, Kirael. Why do Lightworkers need to amass?

KIRAEL: You, the Lightworkers, may not want to hear this, but you have little choice in the matter, for it has to do with the movement into the Great Shift. This is all explained in my first book, *Kirael: The Great Shift*. As you know, you are headed into a new millennium, and everything has begun to escalate. Escalation is what you are experiencing. Turn on your TV and you can see it. I see it around the world. It is escalating, but it is different this time.

This is the exciting part: Why do Lightworkers need to amass? Because before, when the impassioned so-called "powers that be" implemented their thoughts into the system, you, the Lightworkers, were so depressed within your own light that you did not bother challenging those forces. But now, because you are not quite as cloaked in ego as you were in the past, it is up to you, the Lightworkers, to keep the light lit, even for those who do not profess to be Lightworkers. It is not always necessary to be in a challenging stance; it is enough for Lightworkers to understand more clearly that something is not necessarily so just because someone in power says it is.

Yes, you the Lightworkers need to amass. There needs to be little pockets of Lightworkers, so to speak, wherever you go. In this way, like the grass, when one little clump of grass hears something, it can pass it on to the next little clump, and then it gets passed right around the world. This is important because one group might not receive or hear the message. For instance, as we speak, there is a collective energy of Lightworkers creating a situation where action is being taken against the government of Japan for their policies on whale hunting. And the interesting part is that most of them do not know they are Lightworkers.

The reason I emphasize that they do not know they are Lightworkers is because what they are doing through sanctions is only a partial solution to the problem. These people think that because they were successful in getting their government to place sanctions against another government, they have done what they came here to do. True Lightworkers know that is not the answer. True Lightworkers will look within countries such as Japan to find the Lightworkers there. They will support the groups of Lightworkers in Japan, and those in Australia and Alaska will do the same. With intent, all the Lightworkers will begin to amass in this same vibration. Thus, what happens is the guy with his finger on the trigger of the whaling harpoon is affected just like that blade of grass. And maybe, just maybe, he misses every other shot, perhaps without even knowing why.

That is why Lightworkers must amass. It isn't about depending on the government to take care of the ills of the Earth plane. It is about the light energies, the Lightworkers, learning to create a space which, through harmonically engineered light processing and through the amassing of prayers and meditation, moves out in love. Remember your Creator is Love. And in that, everything becomes cured. Everything is healed.

Lightworkers and the Earth Matrix

Can you comment on the impact of Lightworkers in the matrix that you discussed in "Kirael Volume II: The Genesis Matrix"?

KIRAEL: As we in the Guidance Realm understand the Earth plane today, everything in the matrix is being stretched to a new vibration. Those who operate fully within the matrix, which, sad to say, is most of the human world, are now becoming aware that something is different. The world is moving into a state of consciousness that is unstoppable at this point, and it is about the Lightworkers amassing in collective awareness. Lightworkers are known for their ability to choose with their hearts on any subject matter.

You must realize, however, that it is in the best interest of certain powers still prominent in the Earth plane to maintain an unhealed society. For instance, much of your money is spent on the repair of the physical body. Billions upon billions of untold dollars are being poured into medical research. If one could literally think themselves into good health, wouldn't that be a bit of a problem for these powers? You in the physical body attempting to attain your light body must keep in mind that no one answer fits all. For instance, when you listen to my words along with five other people, there will be six different interpretations. What is the point? The point is that from the light world, we direct our vibration into your core essence; we allow you to make your own decisions with guidance. This is why we are called *guides*.

In the world of soy products, for example, people have been using soy for years to better their health. They have been eating soy products such as tofu to bring more strength, more energy, and more enlightenment into their cellular system. This is, however, contrary to what the unseen forces of the matrix energy want you to believe. For this reason, you have recently been hearing in the news that tofu is not as beneficial to the body as believed. Check with your heart for the answer. We are trying from the Guidance Realm to "amass" the Lightworkers, not to influence their decisions but to allow them to receive a higher vibration of the facts.

Lightworkers can make a difference in the world by coming together in collective consciousness. Therefore, you haven't come here this evening to have your decisions made for you. You have come to hear the expressions of a light being; then we hope you will choose to do your own research. At the end of your research, you will not be taking the word of your news press, but you will be taking the word of your inner guidance.

Let's move along and talk about the different things that are happening worldwide. You may not know how far the Earth plane has moved since the great planetary alignment of May 5, 2000. It is awakening to a great awareness. My friends, we have now reached a space in time to move forward in light, or, should you choose, to go deep into the matrix and never be heard from again.

What does this matrix offer? The matrix offers a very safe and secure space of energy. Naturally, the masses still belong to the matrix, and only a small number have discovered the world outside of this matrix. Those that have found the outer world of the matrix choose to share very little of their discoveries with those in the matrix, mostly in fear of criticism. Nevertheless, those who now journey beyond the matrix have begun to know that answers of truth are found in that realm beyond the matrix.

The answers of truth come when you accept guidance from your own spirit and not from some outside force. There are those right now who are on the verge of turning their life over to spirit completely. What I mean to say is: If your spirit says do it, then do it; if it says no, then don't. Is this a bit on the radical side? Well, it might be, my friends, but what you don't know is that you are all in that position anyway because your higher selves are exercising control of this process. The difference between Lightworkers and matrix workers is that matrix workers do not listen to their higher selves. They react to outside influences, whereas Lightworkers listen and interact with their higher selves.

It is for your heart to know what truth is. That is the journey. It is not the journey of the Lightworker to make a decision because somebody says so. It is about following your inner guidance and the guidance of your higher selves. Lightworkers are those who pray, meditate, and believe in love. They believe that love is the only answer to our existence.

Lightworkers amassing is a reality. Lightworkers amassing within this society called the matrix is even more of a reality. The only thing you have is your connection to your truth, or your higher self. By understanding that you are a Lightworker within the matrix and not a matrix worker, you do not have to be held so tightly in the matrix energy. In truth, you need to heal the matrix energy, and the only way to do this is to amass as Lightworkers.

As Lightworkers amass, there will be suppression and oppression when you become too boisterous. This is what happened with the Falun Gong in China. They came, they sat, they were willing to be arrested, even to go to jail. They were willing to die because they were without fear of death. The truth is you will not die unless it is the will of your own higher self to make that a reality. So the Falun Gong in China had the right idea, and chose to make a statement with it. As they chose to make a statement, they all stood on the sidewalk and pointed to a leader. At that point, they became vulnerable because, according to the old way of thinking, all you have to do is cut off the head of the snake and it dies. However, Lightworkers amassing have no head to cut off because they are amassing in light.

Our words are gathering great force on the Earth plane. I don't know if those of you in this circle today have any idea how widely these ideas are being spread. They are being copied on an hourly basis somewhere in the world. Like my work, they are being translated into other languages and transmitted through many different media. There are now many people looking and searching, not just for our work, but for the works of other awakened Lightworkers. So I think we are beginning to do the task that we were sent to do. It leads from one level to the next.

Building Steps or Arriving?

I have heard you say that completion is just a stepping stone in evolution. Can you elaborate on what this means for Lightworkers?

KIRAEL: Yes, there are those who are seeking completions in their lives. They understand that each completion of a task, which usually means that a lesson plan has been learned, is simply a stepping stone in evolution.

In essence, completion in and of itself does not exist, for completion is merely one action leading to the beginning of another interaction.

Let's talk about this interaction. When you set a goal that you would like to complete, look at it as though you are standing before a ten-foot scaffold. On top of the scaffold is the end of the journey, your destination. So there sits your goal, ten feet above you. Up until now, you would build steps. The old way was to plan your way into this space. That was the first thing you would do—build steps, each being one foot in height. Now, the reason the top plateau seems high is because you are thinking like a human.

In your mind, you think you have ten one-foot steps, each one appearing to be higher and more difficult to reach than the one before. Because of old beliefs, you expect that with each step you must work harder. This is how you have classified your evolution up until this very moment. Those steps you have created are there for one reason only—to reinforce that which you know as fear. Because of fear, you hold onto your ego system, pretend that you don't know what is truly on that plateau, and forget your reason to climb. If you went beyond the ego system and the matrix for your answers, you would see what is truly there. You choose instead to take these small, labored steps to arrive at the top of the plateau, and in so doing, slow down your journey.

As you slowly proceed, each step brings you closer to the understanding of this fear, thereby making each step appear higher and higher, thus creating more chaos with each step. Often you find that by the time you are at the top step and are about to reach that new plateau, fear has simply overwhelmed you. So you turn around and jump back down to the bottom and start over again. What you tend to then do is build six-inch steps which make it a little easier to take, but a lot longer to reach the plateau. It becomes a never-ending journey.

The new millennium, my friends, cannot and will not tolerate such energy usage. In the new millennium, you shall not take steps to move to each plateau. You will simply decide the level and you will arrive. In the new millennium, time moves at a quicker pace. Your illusionary scheduling of time will have diminished. As an example, within the first sixty days of your new millennium, time will be compressed anywhere from 10% to 15%.

The reason I bring this up is because I want you to know that the new millennium energy is a collective consciousness. It is that same collective conscious awareness that will move you into this new space. Those of you who have a habit of step-building are about to change your ways. Those who are evolving will not have time to wait for the step-builders. In essence, the Lightworker will have learned to move from plateau to plateau, experiencing things never before thought possible, and it will be most exciting.

I am addressing the Lightworkers of the world (and I assume you are because you are reading these words). You have gone beyond your fears, and you will move by leaps and bounds through the different possibilities that your universe offers you.

So that is the new millennium as I see it unfold. As it unfolds, you will come to the clarity that it is time for change.

The Collective Consciousness

I really enjoyed the metaphor of the Lightworkers and the grass. Isn't that related to the power of collective consciousness?

KIRAEL: That *is* the power of collective consciousness. So let's take that a step further. The power of collective consciousness is brightened or dimmed by the collective awareness of the human light vibration. While the trees hold a constant vibrational level and the animals maintain a constant level for the most part, the human being does not. You see, the human collective consciousness is tainted by what we often refer to as *the ego*. How "in-densified" or how thick your ego veils are usually determines how much light is going to pass through it. Thus, the process of recognizing the power of the collective consciousness is dependent upon the ability of the people to relate to higher vibrations of light. Essentially, Lightworkers have to align themselves with the higher vibrations of the collective consciousness. To do that, Lightworkers move beyond the ego by raising their vibrations above the matrix field to where they are able to align themselves fully in light. Although much of that light will be disheveled upon re-entering the matrix when it returns through the ego system of each individual, it still arrives in a brighter vibration than when it left. And that vibration of light, like the grass we spoke of, affects every human being on Earth.

Through a ripple effect, every thought that you have will in some way affect every person on this planet. You may ask, "To what level?" It may not be very discernable, but it will affect them nevertheless, because every conscious thought you have is empowered through light vibration. If you add sound vibration to a thought, then it is doubly transferred because a sound affects the vibration of the sound, which in turn affects every other vibration of the sound, and so it ripples out.

Any thought that you have has, in its own light, a life. Here in the Beauty [the Honolulu Church of Light], when one person is having a bad day and is thinking, "This isn't good and that isn't good," that energy is literally moving throughout the Beauty. It vibrates within the system of every person here. Let's look at this like the metaphor of the cut grass. Let's say the medium is working in his office, and suddenly someone in the downstairs part of the sanctuary has a tiff with a caller on the telephone and

BOOM! The medium sitting at his desk is like the blade of grass. BOOM! It hits him, sometimes without conscious awareness, and as a Lightworker, he automatically raises his energy for growth. This is just an example of how the ripple effect can cause mass concern.

It is All an Illusion

The word "illusion" comes from the Latin word "inludere" which means to be "in play." Is that what God is doing here?

KIRAEL: It might be seen that way, my friend. This is what I have been trying to tell you from the beginning. It is all just one giant play in evolutionary consciousness.

Then why are we so serious about everything?

KIRAEL: Because you have a great recognition of fear, but as you the Lightworker choose to move forward in the new millennium, you will no longer experience it so fully.

As you eradicate your fears, you will discover this world abounds with new experiences of love and wondrous relationships to enjoy. And only then will you recognize that you have a choice not to experience energy fraught with so much light that it becomes darkened. Only then will you choose to let yourself be free of fear. Instead of running away, you will stand and face your fear, and it will dissipate into your light—because you will have discovered love.

How is light the same as darkness?

KIRAEL: When you look at energy which you consider to be darkness, you need to understand that everything exists from the Light of the God Creator. Similarly, if you are in a space of yin-yang duality, to like, you have to hate. In order to have light, darkness must exist. Therefore, in order to create darkness from the Light of the Creator, it has to be amassed so thickly that it takes on the appearance of darkness. In truth, from light particles tightly compressed together comes the illusion of darkness.

Do I understand that as Lightworkers' fears begin to diminish, there may be an increase in chaos within the masses of humanity?

KIRAEL: I am afraid so [sigh]. Yes, that big sigh I made is because it is pretty much a fact that chaos will be evident. My friends, please listen carefully: If you go back to the earlier question and recognize that you are in play and that it is all just an illusion, then you will fall prey to the chaos only as far as you need to. Hopefully, you won't need to at all.

When I was recently asked by my medium, "Kirael, will the human population ever accept you for who you are?" I answered, "If they accept me as you do, then we will have won the entirety of the Creator's conceptual illusion."

Closing Statement

The day will come when you arrive back into the etheric fabric, or home, as many are understanding it. You will immediately say, as you have done every other time, "I'm so sorry, Kirael. I should've said this or that." And I will tell you the same thing as I have told you in the past, "Get past it. Have your fun over here. Have a good time. We understand that you are doing the best you can as a human." Understand as well, that each of you here has to come to an understanding that your mission will come to closure when you recognize your Creator Light again. Indeed, each time you have had the opportunity to recognize your Creator Light, you have immediately volunteered to come back here and finish the job.

My friends, it is the beauty of evolution that emerges not always as victorious, but as light. If it emerges as light, then there is nothing more you would want. The beauty of light is your existence. Your existence is the light.

Good evening, my friends.

2 CONCEPTION TO BIRTH: YOUR JOURNEY OF AWARENESS IN THE WOMB

Opening Statement

KIRAEL: Good evening.

Looks like we have quite a nice group here tonight to talk about the beginnings of your life here on the Earth plane. And when we talk about the life of the Earth being, believe me, it is quite different from life on other planes of understanding. So let us begin with an opening statement and I think we shall have a grand time.

It is said that the beautiful particles of the Creator Light simply float about until they connect with one another and begin a thing called *life*. Let us suppose there is this one single particle floating throughout the entire understanding of the world of Light. It has lived many lives to become aware of all the energy that exists. And once again, the Creator has called upon this light being and asked if it would journey to the Earth plane to begin a new life. Oh, the little particle is so excited, so happy. It is so honored that the Creator would acknowledge its existence. It recognizes being part of the vastness of the Creator. Still, how could one single light particle be ever so fortunate to have the Creator's full awareness focused on it?

It has waited for so long to be given this grand opportunity to journey as a human again, for it knows that billions upon billions of particles of the Creator Light, more than there is even a name for, desire nothing more, nothing less, than to make a journey here to this place called Earth. Each and every one welcomes the privilege of living the life of a human, of being loved in the five senses, and being able to smell, and touch, and taste, and see all the beauty that can come with it. And here now is the chance.

Thus, the little particle begins planning this new journey. It thinks of all of the other times that it has been here on the Earth plane—how many beautiful lives it has had, how many exciting times have been available to it. "What will I do this time?" the light particle ponders. "Well, I've had so many great lives," it says. "I've had the grand lives of different processes—some poor, some rich. I've been happy. I've been sad. Let me look through all of those lifetimes and decide the life plan best suited for my evolution now." Then the program is discovered; the blueprint is made. The little light particle knows what life plan it wants to go through in its next lifetime on Earth.

Now comes one of the most exciting parts of the journey. The Creator opens up all heavens and all lights. It says unto the particle, "You may begin now by choosing those whom you wish to be born to." So it looks at the plan and thinks, "Let's see. Good gracious, I've done a bunch of poor lives, so I think I'm going to pick me some parents that are really, really wealthy this time." Well, you can't blame the particle, can you? Each and every one of you exists as one of these beautiful particles of Light and each of you has got choices, right?

Let us imagine that you are that light particle. Now you start looking at a whole number of people that are in the process of considering whether or not to have a baby. You start narrowing the possibilities down, until finally, you find a couple that looks really good. You think this couple can really offer everything that fits in the lesson plans for your life.

I might add that you are not allowed to be overly selective at this point. As a light particle, you can set the general, more basic parts of the framework of your blueprint. You simply know you are going to make the journey, you select your parents, and you decide on a female or male life, or a very balanced life, or an "I'm-not-particular" type of life.

Oh, there are your soon-to-be parents. You know what they are doing. You can feel their vibration from where you are in spirit form. You are just as happy as can be because you know the Truth of the Creator. You know there is no separation between you and this awesome Essence. You are the Creator and everything is just beautiful. Mom and Dad come together in a blissful moment and it all begins. You are ready. You watch. There is the beautiful little egg, and here comes a little river of sperm making its way down the track. Possibly, you have planned to be a female this time. Then, lo and behold! The little bugger that slides in there is a male, Y-chromosome. You say, "Well, that's all right. I can work with that. Not a problem at all," because at that very moment, you are conceived, and your life begins.

Let's back up a minute, because here is where it gets interesting. If I asked each and every person in the room today what they thought the most predominant fear of the human world was, do you suppose I might hear the word *dying*? That's right; the fear of dying is one of the biggest fears Earth beings have. Do you know why? Because the moment that sperm and that egg come together, you—who until this moment have been floating serenely in the Creator's energy—experience a sense of separation. As your core light essence enters the fertilized egg, you feel as if you have in some way just died.

But, you say, aren't we talking about a birth process? Yes, we are. Still, for a brief moment you do think, "I've lost my Creator. Wow, what happened? There was this big boom and here I am. And now, I am a part of this little process that's taking place." It doesn't take very long for you to figure out that everything is all right after that. Hence, we have now answered the question, When does life begin on Earth?

So here you are—conceived, brand-new and feeling grand. As you adjust to being in your mother's womb, you faintly recall that this part of the human journey lasts about nine months. But wait! You have just experienced a sense of separation from your Creator. And after nine months, you are going to feel separation again—this time from your mother. When does all this separation stop? The feeling of separation becomes part of your reality.

The First Nine Months

So here you are for nine months in a beautiful world. You are all snuggled in this beautiful liquid world, starting to put all of the pieces together.

Month 1. In the first thirty days of your life, you don't spend much time with Mom. In fact, you are pretty much ignoring Mom because you have other things to do. You have to start putting the life plan that you brought with you into some semblance of order, and you are not going to do it floating around in your mommy's belly. Instead, you spend most of your time connected to an umbilical cord, riding through what we consider to be the etheric fabric and meeting up with all of the angels, the guides and all the other beautiful energies available to you. Essentially, you spend the first thirty days staying as connected to God Creation as you possibly can.

Month 2. As you roll into the second month, you feel a duality process. There is an increasingly separate part of you. It is saying, "You must conform to the energy force that you have entered into. You must begin to experience this process called human." You still want to be spirit, yet you are beginning to feel your body forming. Primarily, at this stage, you are adjusting and resetting your energies, making sure that you have everything in the proper working order so that you can experience the journey laid out in your lesson plans.

Month 3. Then the real fun begins. After two months in contact with Mom, you are now able to sense her on a much higher level. You know her energies very well by now: you can feel her heart, because it is your heart; you can feel her pulse, because it is your pulse. And everything is just becoming hunky-dory betwixt you and Mom.

So there you are, trying to get yourself all squeezed into that body while Mom is still pretty active. She still thinks she can run, jog, dance, and do all these other things. For you, every one of those little bounces keeps you rocking back and forth in your little liquid world, just as happy as you can be.

Towards the middle of the third month, you begin to sense a second voice. This other voice is really deep; it rumbles and growls. It says things like, "Are you in there? Are you really in there?" That is Dad. And Dad can be a real pain because you remember these noises from other lifetimes. Your relationship with Dad begins; you are developing the ability to recognize voices and listen to conversations. You cannot hear Dad too clearly, but you hear Mom well, especially through her thoughts.

Month 4. At four months, your hearing sensors are being formed and you hear beautifully. There are even headphones today that can be put on Mommy's belly so the baby can hear music. So parents need to remember that if the sound is too loud, it causes a lot of discomfort in there. Be gentle if you are going to play music to your unborn infant.

By four months, you are having complete thought transference with both Mom and Dad. When Mom thinks, "Oh, God, I think I'm going to throw up again," you are thrilled, especially when you feel a whoosh like a roller-coaster ride. You think it is great.

Dad gets involved, too. You sense him thinking one night when all of you are lying in bed, "What does it cost to send him to a private school? I've got to put him through college... How much tuition will I have to pay?" All the while, you are thinking, "Tuition...what's tuition?" You are trying to catch these thought transfers and figure out your own thinking process. "What does all this mean? Does that mean he doesn't like me? Am I really just about this thing called money?"

Thought transference is definitely taking place, and it goes both ways. Remember, you have been human before and have accumulated many human experiences. So when you hear Mom thinking, "I just need to sit down and have a nice bowl of saimin [noodle soup]," it gets you thinking, "Yeah, with a scoop of chocolate ice cream in it." Then Mom goes, "I don't know why, but all of the sudden, I want a scoop of chocolate ice cream in my saimin." [*laughter*] (People on the mainland are going to have trouble with saimin, aren't they?) In any case, Mom seems to be going crazy at this point, craving ice cream with her saimin.

Month 5. The fifth month is an exciting time. It is the time that the Creator is still in total contact with you and reminds you that you are a bundle of love. That is all you are: love, love and more love. You start snuggling up to Mommy's backbone, reaching up, seeing if you can touch things. Unfortunately for Mom, you make her think you are doing handsprings inside of her because you simply want to experience everything. The fifth month is a thrilling time for you; the human life is your life now and you are more than halfway through the nine months. So you go through this period of love, where everything is love, on top of love.

Month 6. Then you go into the sixth month, and guess what? At this point, you have mastered being in Mom's space and grow more curious about the world outside the womb. You are thinking, "How do I get out of here? I can hear Dad's voice. I can hear Mom laughing. I heard Mom cry last night. That didn't make me feel good, so I cried inside with her. But then I heard laughter and I heard people talking. Oh, wow, I've got sisters and brothers, and I can't wait to meet them. I have mastered this thing called pregnancy, and I don't want to do it anymore. God, can I get out of here now?" And guess where that takes you?

Month 7. It takes you right into the seventh month. If you follow my numerology, you know that the number 7 takes you to transition, a space of transition. If you had to pick a month when the child truly recognizes its spirituality, it is the seventh month, for that is when you spend a great deal of time with the Creator again. You travel back and forth, more than before, transitioning from your ethereal self to the human reality. Until that time, you liked to stay with Mom a lot, enjoying Mom's energy pattern, her love, her laughter, her crying, and the funny stuff she eats. But the seventh month is mainly reserved for the Creator's Light. [See a full description of Kirael's Numerology in *Kirael Volume II: The Genesis Matrix.*]

Month 8. Everything is moving right along when you move into the eighth month. This is where the likelihood of turning back is well beyond anything you can do. You have stretched poor Mom out into oblivion. She looks like she is all puffed up in the center. She groans when she tries to stand up. GGGGRRRRR. That is what you feel when Mom goes, "Ohhhh," but to you inside, it sounds more like GGGGRRRRR with an echo chamber effect. You like that sound so much that as soon as Mom settles down and gets all comfortable again, you kind of wiggle to make her get up again. Then you get to feel the GGGGRRRRR again. Mom may have reached a point where she has lost just about all her humor, but it is still a laugh a minute for you. It is so much fun that you can't help yourself!

Most women will recognize the baby is in constant motion at that time, for whatever reason. I think it is because you have been having a great time with everything you do. If Mom sits and shifts from hip to hip, well, that tips you in a certain direction. Oh, you just love that, except you get bored really fast, so you make Mom tip back the other way. It is like a form of communication between Mom and you.

Much of the eighth month is used to complete any final adjustments of your blueprint or life plans. You also lose some of your ability to consciously travel between the ethereal and physical worlds in that month. Your angels, however, do remain in constant watchfulness to assist you in your completion schedule.

Month 9. First, the ninth month is no picnic for either the mom or the baby. Up to this point, you have had things exactly the way you wanted. You have had everything in your favor, and Mom and Dad have taken excellent care of you. So has your doctor, although you don't much care for his probing around.

Indeed, the entire journey to this point has been an absolute thrill for you because you have been fully aware since the second month, which is when your thinking as an adult human began. Yes, that is right; your thoughts at two months in the womb are just like the thoughts you are having here tonight.

At the ninth month, your wiggle room is gone. In fact, ever since the eighth month, every time you stick your arm straight out, your mom goes, "Ohhh," and by this time, you have become a little tired of hearing that. You even try to hold a little stiller so that Mom doesn't become antisocial with you and say such things as, "Oh, I can't wait to get this thing out of here."

So here we are—completion is at hand. You are thinking it is going to be so awesome. Then the thought hits you, "Wait a minute. I've been born before. Oh no, I'm turning upside down. I don't want to do that." Then there is a narrow passage, a tunnel before you. There is light at the end of the tunnel, and you are saying, "Oh, my God, transition is upon me," and you head for the light.

Can you imagine? A five- or six-pound baby looking at that tunnel and thinking, "I'm going through there? I don't think so. Maybe I'll just stay back here and live here for the rest of my life." But Mom is having no part of that; Dad is having no part of it. Most of all, the Creator is not having any part of that. You have a journey to do. You put in for this mission.

The next thing you do is move towards the light. Now don't confuse this light with the light in another transition process. In that case, people see a light, head for it, and return back into the Creator's Light. This is a different light; what you are seeing is the light of the Earth plane.

And suddenly, the little tunnel gets relatively large, and out you come— final transition, completion. You realize immediately that you have just left one level of life and entered into another. You have just made your newest transition after nine months of life. And so it begins again, all brand-new.

I ask you here to remember one important thing, my friends: the journey of pregnancy is an absolute gift from the Creator. What takes place in those nine months is the most intricate part of a baby's existence. At the moment the egg and the sperm connect, the God Light particle enters the cell and the

Trinity of Truth, Trust, and Passion is formed. This is what takes you from the Light pattern of the God Creator Itself into the physical world.

Questions & Answers

Your Birth Name

What is the importance of a birth name?

KIRAEL: Did you know that you normally choose your birth name in the first month in the womb? Most parents sometimes go about changing that, however. Sometimes an "Abraham" ends up being a "Timmy." The truth is, babies have a pretty intricate system for picking out a name. They go by vibration, basing the name on such factors as the vibrational energies of the mother and father and the life plan decided on.

I would like to suggest here that you let the unborn child choose its own name. How, you may ask? First, the baby will try to use phonetic sounds to communicate the name to the mother by thought transference. When the mother doesn't get it, the baby will send out spurts of energetic thought in hopes that Dad will help pick the name. If you are a metaphysical family, it is probably a little easier because somebody in the family should be able to pick up on the name.

Let us hope you are these really great parents who are expecting a baby. So when you get the name, please honor your unborn child by using the name it has selected. The vibration of whatever name chosen is going to guide everything that the baby does, especially in the first six-and-a-half to seven years of life. It is going to be the way people approach the child. Many things are going to be guided by that name.

When you are the particle light planning to come to the Earth plane, you try your best to set up everything as well as you can. All the choices you make to get over here are perfectly laid out for the life that you plan to experience, and there are no exceptions to that rule, my friend. This even includes the choice of birth name.

Did I understand correctly that the vibrational essence of our names is connected with our lesson plans?

KIRAEL: Yes, because your name is a vibration that you live with throughout your life.

So if I have a feeling that I want to change my name, it means I also change my vibration. Does it also mean that I change my lesson plan?

KIRAEL: Absolutely. You may have lived on the Earth plane thirty-five, forty, fifty, or whatever number of years, and you wake up one morning and think your name should be changed to Aretha. Everybody knows your name is Sue or Patti, but you think your name should be Aretha. When you tell people you know this, many will not understand.

Then one day you walk into a beautiful little church like the Honolulu Church of Light and say to one of the ministers, "I've decided to change my name. My new name is Aretha." And they say, "Oh, that is such a perfect name for you!" and you think, "You see? I knew it." Well, Aretha was actually the name you chose coming into this lifetime, but your Mom and Dad didn't listen to you. They couldn't understand that the name Aretha would bring out your highest resonant form. Eventually, however, many people do grow up and change their names. This way, they find the vibration that they first intended to experience in this lifetime.

It is traditional in our society, as it is in many other societies, for women to assume the last name of the husband when they get married. How does this fit in the lesson plan?

KIRAEL: I am about to make a lot of women unhappy and a lot of men unhappier here. There is absolutely no reason for you to switch names in the middle of your life. Switching boats in the middle of the stream doesn't make any sense, does it? Then why would you switch the name?

Whenever you change your name, you change the resonant factor of your vibration. Hence, the best thing would be to keep the name you were born with to maintain the resonant factor of your life plan. If you want another name, you can adjust the change that you are about to make by adding it onto your birth name. But when you drop one name and pick up another, you do, in fact, alter part of your life plan. This may seem a minor thing, but it is important.

Your Birth Number

Is there also a number, like your name, that you decide on for its vibrational frequency?

KIRAEL: Every one born on the Earth plane has a number that ties it to spirit, to its higher self. The moment your particle light makes connection with the sperm and egg, you have a number that will resonate with you for your entire life. The resonant number for you, for instance, [addressing the person asking the question] is the number 8. When you were conceived, the number of your blueprint was registered an 8, which is the number that evolves in and out of the dimensional processes.

Adjustments to the Original Life Plan

What happens to a baby in the womb that is feeling a lot of conflict between the parents which was not part of the original life plan? Would that conflict be added to the life plan?

KIRAEL: It is added to the blueprint, yes. Let's say there is an unplanned pregnancy and Mom is extremely ecstatic about it. Dad, on the other hand, is opposed to it, or is even unaware of the pregnancy. Well, part of the blueprint has now shifted. If you recall what I said earlier, the baby is still spending much of the time in the Creator's Light in the first month, but everything is logged into the system, right? Everything that Mom thinks, every conversation and every sound element that comes through Mom, is picked up by the new baby and adjustments are made.

Can you explain further about the light particle that carries the vibrational frequency of the life plan into the fertilized egg?

KIRAEL: Surely. The blueprint that you bring at the time of conception is aligned to spirit. When the God Light particle enters into this new life that is formed between the egg and the sperm, you see a new trinity formation, which is the key to the matrix system. It carries the magical plan, or the blueprint, that is designated by your higher self to guide you through your human life.

Be clear, my friend, that the blueprint is always changeable. It is like having a set of blueprints for a house you plan to build with five bedrooms. But in the midst of the construction, you might decide to change it to four bedrooms and one den. Likewise, you have nine months to reset the blueprint and that can be done in just about any way that you want.

Here is another example. Let us suppose that in selecting your mom and dad, you chose to have parents who are very wealthy. However, in about the third month after you are conceived, there is an unexpected drop in the stock market and the set of parents you chose are no longer rich. That doesn't mean you end the plan of a luxurious life, only that you begin to readjust the blueprint. You can continue to work on this blueprint in the nine months that you are held within the womb and then create your own wealth thereafter.

Masterminding with the Unborn Child

I have a question about babies and masterminding. You were saying that in the fourth month a baby can communicate its thoughts to the parents. Can parents mastermind with the baby while it is in the womb? (More on Masterminding in Chapter 6, "The Four Pillars of Conscious Creation.")

KIRAEL: Good question. Up to the fourth month in the womb, the baby vibrates more to statements than to questions that the parents might make. In the first month of pregnancy, for example, if Mom and Dad are saying things such as, "This child is going to be a genius. He's going to play the piano. He's going to sing. He's going to dance…," the child is registering all of this in the blueprint. It is all being coded in. Conversely, if the parents are saying, "I hope the baby is not like your Uncle Bob. He's a dweeb…," that, too, is being registered in the blueprint. It is registering, "Is this what I am supposed to do…to be like him?"

Statements have powerful endings and are therefore more easily picked up by the baby. Hence, they are automatically registered in the blueprint. Questions are not so readily registered because they are open-ended and without clear resolution.

Can that affect the original blueprint that the particle is bringing with it?

KIRAEL: Surely, because remember, the blueprint is being worked on now. You may have decided in your original blueprint on a female body but you get a male body instead, so you need to change the blueprint. Most of these changes are being done etherically up until the fourth month. Put it this way: many changes can be made in the first month, quite a few in the second, a few in the third, but by the fourth month, the blueprint starts to be quite set. After that the changes become a little harder to make.

Gender and the Blueprint

Can you explain further about what happens when you may have decided on a female lesson plan in your blueprint but a Y-chromosome comes in at the moment the egg, the sperm and the particle of Light come together?

KIRAEL: That is one of the more traumatic spaces of your life. By that time, you have already chosen your parents, and you have your male or female lesson plans all lined up in your blueprint. (That is, unless you have reached a very old soul age where it no longer makes a difference whether you are male or female.)

If you planned on a female life plan, but the plan changed to male at the moment of conception, the blueprint is still wide open and it can be adjusted. In most cases, you don't change the blueprint. It remains intact and you just add to the blueprint. You might think about it this way: No matter the plan you have, if you live life to the fullest in love and continue your healing process all the way, it will not make any difference what your gender is. The body will fit the plan. That is always the case. Not only that, but the plan perfectly fits the body. Ultimately, there are no mistakes.

The Veils of the Ego

When the baby is in the womb, it has no ego. How is the ego system set in place?

KIRAEL: The ego system sets itself in place when the mother's water bag breaks just prior to being born. When the baby realizes that it will soon leave the comfort, the love and the light of the womb, something new arises. At that precise moment, the ego is set in place and the remembrance of fear is real.

The veils of the ego are the thickest at the moment of birth, largely because the Creator does not want you to change your mind at this stage. For this same reason, the baby does not feel the birthing pains that the mother feels. This is an agreement made between baby and mother. The ego acts as a protective device to shield the baby from the trauma of birth and separation. However, the veils begin to diminish soon after birth. All it takes is feeling the warmth of the mother's breast and hearing Dad say, "I love you." It works even without words. Just thoughts of love allow the veil of the ego to relax its tight grip as the newborn begins its new journey outside the mother's womb.

Despite all this, the ego becomes almost non-existent in the first twenty-four hours of life. This is to allow the blueprint to be downloaded into the newly activated parts of the brain. Yes, the brain functions differently in the womb than it does out of the womb. So parents, hear me words! Talk to that child constantly in the first twenty-four hours. I don't care if you don't get any sleep. Simply talk to that child, or at least sleepstate program your thoughts into the child if you need to sleep. This is vitally important because the first twenty-four hours of life is the most accessible and impressionable time in a newborn's life. [Sleepstate Programming is one of the Four Pillars of Conscious Creation which Kirael discusses in Chapter 6.]

When I gave birth to my first child, hospitals were still keeping newborn babies separated from their mothers for long periods of time immediately following birth. Therefore, I could not hold my baby very much. Is there trauma for the child as a result of this?

KIRAEL: Absolutely. If this information had been known forty years ago, the world would be better off today, because the ego system that aligns at birth needs to be nurtured, and then nurtured even more, considering the baby has just experienced its first moments of fear and separation.

It is important to understand that when the baby exits the womb, it begins to align its energies with all of the energy forces of the new matrix that it has entered. And when the newborn does not have physical contact with its mother, it feels a very strong sense of separation. Thus it is left to look for its mother etherically, and that is not as easy as it might sound for a newborn child. You might think, "But wait a minute. All they know is Mom, so they should be able to find her easily." However, the heavy energy placed upon it by the density of the matrix begins to interfere with the baby's sixth sense. That is why a baby needs to be held and nurtured by the mother as much as possible.

How many times does the ego system change in the first year, and when does that occur?

KIRAEL: In the first year, the ego system changes four times. If you were to watch a child change egos, you would see it happen approximately once every three months. Actually, that isn't so bad, because in year three, you will see twelve ego system changes!

Naturally, the changes vary with the parents. If the parents are very wisdom-filled, very spiritual, very oriented to Light, then they can help the child's ego adjust easily through each change. Parents can support the child by conversing more and being more loving with the child during those times. Remember, when you left the Creator's Light, you felt separation. When you left the womb, you felt separation again. With every ego adjustment, the child fears another separation. So, loving attention to your child will help the process along greatly.

Babies Born by Cesarean Section

Are babies that are born by the cesarean process missing out on something?

KIRAEL: Actually, the choice to be born in that manner is usually part of a blueprint, for it knows the mother cannot deal with the natural birth process. If a cesarean birth was not planned, the blueprint will be adjusted to accommodate it. If the baby discovers, for instance, that the mother will be too traumatized by natural birth or that the mother's bone structure does not allow her to give birth naturally, the child will adjust the birth plan to allow a different reality focus. This is necessary as the veil is different when the baby is born by cesarean section. Meaning, the veil carries a different vibration for a C-section experience than the veil for natural birth.

Is there a correlation between babies born by cesarean section and colicky tendencies?

KIRAEL: Being colicky simply means that the baby is confused at its arrival. They made the plan. They are doing the blueprint, but they are thinking, boy, did they mess things up. They are already on the Earth plane, but they have no escape hatches set up. They have got to do the whole process, and they are downright aggravated. Their ego isn't working well enough. They can still see the other side, but at the same time, they are looking on this side and hearing their Mom say, "Goo-goo, gah-gah." They are thinking, "I know Mom can repeat the words to 'The Star Spangled Banner' backwards and forwards…and she is telling me, 'Goo-goo, gah-gah?' Mom is really upsetting me now. Let me show her gah-gah how things work!" Then the baby starts talking. It talks and it talks and it talks to Mom, only it comes out as a "Waaaaaa!"

Two Forms of Abortions

In the case of abortion, was there a previously made agreement between the mother and the spirit coming in as a child?

KIRAEL: Well, there are two forms. First, you have what we call an in-service spirit. That means the spirit comes in literally to experience the abortion, and then it returns into the Creator Light to await another assignment. The in-service spirit has agreed with the pregnant mother to be part of her abortion experience. The other form is when the lesson plan did not include the abortion. In such cases, you, the light particle, automatically return into the Light and that is the end of it. Then you reprogram, reset, and pray your little heart out that God will soon give you another opportunity to return to the Earth plane.

There's a lot of controversy in the Christian community about abortion being against God's will and about it being murder. What is Spirit's position on that?

KIRAEL: What I am about to say will not please everyone. There really is no position. The truth is that every spirit has the right to its life no matter what its choices are. Abortion involves all parties having to make individual choices to arrive at a collective decision, and only when the collective decision is made does the abortion take place. Let the point be clear that if the mother decides that she does not wish to carry the child to full term, the baby must have made the agreement to be aborted on the spirit level. Otherwise, adjustments are made in the blueprint, and the mother changes her mind and bears the child. Believe me, the baby has to be in alignment with this process or it does not happen.

Premature Infants

I would like to ask a question concerning premature babies. I gather from what you said earlier that there is a lesson plan for every month in the womb. What happens in terms of a lesson plan when a child is born prematurely at six months? Or is the lesson plan actually completed at six months?

KIRAEL: The answer is yes, the lesson plan is completed at that point. Now if you have a set of parents who are spiritually-inclined or metaphysically aware, they will enlist the spirit world to allow the child to go through the last three months of the pregnancy—even etherically, if necessary. If the parents are aware enough to see that the child needs to experience the seventh, eighth, and ninth month in the womb, they will assist the baby with their love and nurturing. In either case, the baby does fulfill all of the developmental stages it requires and then experiences the birthing process at the proper time.

Is the infant that is born prematurely working on two lesson plans simultaneously—the lesson plan that etherically completes the nine months as well as the new lesson plan that begins at birth?

KIRAEL: Yes. You will notice premature babies are normally placed in incubators, and that is certainly another lesson plan. Have you ever noticed that those babies are usually very, shall we say, "colorful"? Babies that have to spend time in incubators often appear to change colors as they adjust to being out of the womb, while continuing the nine stages of development.

It is also very likely that the child's blueprint called for it to be born prematurely. In any case, the parents can most lovingly support the premature infant with etheric light, or *white light*. Remember, time is an illusion and in that, much is possible.

Adopted Children

I want to ask about children who end up being adopted. How is that arranged and how does that kind of life plan work out where the child may have selected its birth parents but not the adopting parents?

KIRAEL: Well, that is an interesting question, and I will answer it in this manner: If, in fact, it is arranged, then everything is in perfection. If the plan is not arranged that way, the blueprint is radically adjusted.

Let us say that Dad has left, and Mom decides that she simply cannot do it alone. It doesn't mean she doesn't love the child; it just means that she cannot provide for the needs of the baby. So she puts the baby up for adoption. Adoption, as I have said, is the complete re-alignment of the plan, and oftentimes, the child will never be able to accept the adoption fully because the mastermind of the natural parents was not clear. By that I mean, Mom was unclear; she couldn't make a decision and was on again, off again about keeping the baby. In addition, there was no contact with Dad. As a result, the adopted child normally has a lot of trouble straightening out its lesson plan—until about the twenty-first year. Around the twenty-first year—after three sets of seven years, if you understand numerology—the blueprint changes just as it was programmed to do.

Multiple Births

Can you tell us about multiple births?

KIRAEL: If you have twins, you can wind up with what we call a split soul. This occurs with identical twins, where the same soul, by splitting its aspects, can actually reside in both of the twins. Twins are literally tied together in spirit.

Multiple Personalities

I have a question about multiple personalities. Is that something that forms in the womb?

KIRAEL: Very seldom; it is usually done in spirit. What can happen in multiple personalities is that more than one light particle simultaneously enters the egg and the sperm at the moment of conception, but only one survives. Still, multiple personalities, or multiple blueprints remain. [More on this in Chapter 8]

Babies of Mothers on Alcohol or Drugs

What happens to babies in utero when their mothers are involved in alcohol or substance abuse?

KIRAEL: Alcohol and drug abuse on the mother's part always create situations that alter the blueprint of the unborn infant. Alcohol abuse always adjusts the blueprint, sometimes in a radical way. A mother's drug abuse problem seriously alters the life plan of the child, because the 10% mind is being set to function with the 90% mind, or the All That Is, during this time. Drugs actually create breaks in that process, preventing the 10% brain from developing fully on its own. [Kirael speaks more fully on the 10% / 90% awareness in Chapter 6 of *Kirael Volume II: The Genesis Matrix.*]

When you create the life blueprint, you mainly focus on the final outcomes. But when a pregnant woman takes drugs, she magnetically rearranges the brain patterns of that child. In such cases, the child may act perfectly normal for twenty, thirty years, and then bang! Just like that, they slip, so to speak, and nobody knows why. This comes as a result of the breaks in the 10% and 90% segments of the mind and it often takes time to manifest. In most cases, however, birth defects from substance abuse are discovered at birth.

When we talk about babies of mothers who are substance abusers, is that young soul participating in the mother's substance abuse lesson plan or is that something that has been levied upon it without a choice?

KIRAEL: The baby is participating in and feeling the affects of the drugs. If this were not part of the child's blueprint, the child could choose to exit at that point. But what it will normally do is reset its blueprint to try to match up with the mother.

The Absent Father

When a father is not present during the pregnancy, is the unborn child aware of this?

KIRAEL: Absolutely, and far more than most realize. The unborn child has an attachment to the mother. It has thoughts simultaneously with the mother's. When I say "simultaneously," I literally mean that every thought that passes through the mother's mind is simultaneously picked up by the baby in the womb. As for the father, the child will also pick up the father's thoughts, but a fraction of a second later. So if the father is absent during this time, it knows it is missing a large part of its experience. Ultimately, because of a lack of balance, it takes a long time for the child to get over the absence of the father, if ever.

Blueprint Focus: Experiences or Objectives?

I know many of us have different objectives we want to accomplish in our lifetimes, but we also have differing experiences that lead us to those objectives. In designing a blueprint, which would be sacrificed first, the objective or the experience?

KIRAEL: Oh, I don't like to say it, but over here you usually sacrifice the experience. You always go for the objective first. If I were to be a human again, I would choose the experience over the objective because of how it affects the blueprint. For instance, whenever you decide to take a shortcut on any experience that is written in the blueprint, they are all logged in the blueprint as shortcuts. Consequently, when you return home you must reset your next blueprint to include all the missed experiences as a result of all the shortcuts taken.

You see, if you chose to do the experience, the objective would come out the way you wanted it to anyway. And here is where I make a plug for meditation, because those who meditate can be in constant awareness of their blueprint. Through meditation, they are allowed to make adjustments to their blueprint and to bring the objectives and experiences into alignment. This allows people who meditate to recognize the matrix energies they will need to experience in order to reach the chosen objective.

Raising Children

It is said that compassionate parents will let a child stumble and fall when it is learning to walk in order to allow the child to evolve.

KIRAEL: Yes, that is right. If the parents are full-fledged lights of Creation, meaning that they are very spiritually-oriented and aware, then they will create cushion pads of light for their child to fall on. A compassionate parent will pray into the objective of the blueprint of the child, that the child learns how to fall properly; thereby not denying it the experience of the fall, but, hopefully, bringing that experience to the most beautiful completion.

Music and the Unborn Child

Some people believe that playing classical music to the child in the womb stimulates the brain cells. What's the truth about that?

KIRAEL: It doesn't have to be classical music. It can be any music that offers the broadest range of the musical scale. For instance, if you play, thump, thump, thump, thump, it is not enough. Classical music covers all of the musical scale, from the lowest to the highest notes, and it is soft and intertwining. Thus, it is definitely to a child's advantage to hear some classical music.

In contrast, vocal music is a little disconcerting for babies because they are just starting to identify voice patterns while they are in the womb. First, they are learning the voice patterns of Mom and Dad, and if you play a lot of vocal music on the tummy, they follow the voice pattern of the singer. The singer's voice will initially throw them off a bit although they usually adjust to it.

Shift Babies

Do you have any words of wisdom you can share on "shift babies"?

KIRAEL: I would say to the parents, please be aware that your children are shift babies. Shift babies need extra-special care. Many of them are coming in with a lot of angelic energy, a lot of galactic energy, a lot of human energy—all in one package. So you have got to treat your shift babies extra-special. [Kirael explains what Shift Babies are in Chapter 2 of *Kirael: The Great Shift.*]

Closing Statement

I will make this a brief closing statement, if you will. In the love of Light and the All That Is right, I offer to each and every one of you these words, for the vast majority of you came here through some sort of birth process. You do not remember your birth because it is not for you to remember. My concern here, however, is less for those already born; it is more for those energies that are coming in now—the shift babies. They are coming onto the Earth plane in great force now, so prepare yourselves. Be aware of their love and their light shall open up your paths.

Good evening, my friends.

3 THE BLUEPRINT OF LIFE: YOUR FIRST SEVEN YEARS

Opening Statement

KIRAEL: Good evening.

I would like to make it very clear that I have come from across many light centuries and from many different areas of light to make the journey here with the sole purpose of being with you this evening. For each and every one of you who decides to take the journey of awakening, this shall be a very special event. If you are open to what I say tonight, you will begin to allow yourself the awakening point—the quickening, if you will—to the light particles within.

In our last meeting we spoke of the nine-month journey in the womb and about what we call *birth*. Let me see if I can bring that into focus again for you now. First, you were lying there in the warmth and glow of your mother's womb, waiting your turn to come to the Earth plane. Then around the ninth month, the journey of the birthing process began. In those very first moments when you first breathed in the air of the Earth plane, you found that you were no longer a part of the water dimension. You also came to the stunning realization that being born an Earth human meant you could no longer return to the Creator Light in the same manner you did in the womb. And now we speak of the first seven years of Earth life, in hopes that it will give you new meaning to your life today.

The First Seven Years

Year 1. The interesting part in the first year, my friends, is that you are meeting with your angelic guardians and guides to refine and define your blueprint—and all the while, you are stationary here on the Earth plane. This accounts for a newborn infant sleeping so much in that first year, allowing time to travel, refocus, and refine the blueprint.

I will give you an example. If it had been your plan to experience this lifetime in a female body, but lo and behold, you ended up in a male body, this would be one of the first things that you would want adjusted and re-aligned in your life plan. The lesson plans for this lifetime would remain intact, yet the way of achieving them would most likely need to be altered.

In the first year you also become more tuned into your mother and father in a different light; for remember, everything takes on a different focus in the air-breathing world as opposed to the water world of the womb. You no longer see only with the third eye, but with human eyes. You no longer feel the freedom of the light body, experiencing instead the constrictions of a physical body. Your entire cellular consciousness is adjusting to the Earth's vibration.

Parents, if you have a baby that seems to cry a lot in the first year, it is labeled as being "colicky." I think your baby might prefer to call it "regret," having discovered that it cannot simply fly away at any moment as it might want. Each time the baby feels constrained, it tries to remember from seemingly long ago how things work in a body. This means that the first thing the baby wants to do is point at its mother and say, "I'm hungry." Well, you know what sounds come out of the mouth, and you know the finger doesn't naturally point very well. In fact, all five fingers go out at the same time. There is little control of the muscle patterns which were established in the blueprint. All this is a bit disconcerting as the baby ponders how it can move this process along at a more rapid rate. Always is the human experience in a hurry, isn't it?

Because all of you here tonight are humans of the adult world, all of you know that it takes an awfully long illusion of time to be able to get the physical body to do everything that you want it to do, only to discover in later years that it reverts back and refuses to do anything you want it to do again, right? [*laughter*] Oh, yes. Isn't that true? You can tell that those laughing are up there in the aging process.

If you will, let's continue on with this blueprint, because the first year, if you follow my numerology, is what I call "The God Year." This year is when you experience not only a lot of interaction with the Creator's Light but with all of the angelic forces. Most of you know that when you come to the Earth plane, you always bring a guardian with you. Some of you will even bring a pair of guardians with you. Most of you here this evening, by the way, brought a pair of guardian angels with you because you knew this lifetime would be one of those really awesome lifetimes. So you brought in all the help you could get. What you do not remember, however, was that for the first thirty or forty years of your life you would lose sight of your angels and pretend that they did not exist. My friends, if you think it is difficult for you to be here, you should consider the angels' side of the situation. Your guardian angels agreed to come here to be of service to you, only to find out that for the most part, you have ignored them.

What about the ego? As you get more comfortable with your physical body in your first year, the veils of your ego get stronger. You start to close the gaps that allowed you to travel quickly back and forth between the worlds. You spend more and more time in the body process, getting to know your parents better. You use your five senses at a much higher vibration, becoming familiar with how your parents look and smell.

Here is an example for those of you who are planning to have a child. With babies in the first year of their understanding, you want to be extremely delicate with their hands. Located in the very tips of their fingers is a highly activated cellular consciousness with which they scan and maneuver themselves around. Perhaps you have noticed that from the outset newborn infants will always reach out with their hands, seemingly searching for something. What the baby is actually doing is slowing down the use of the third eye (which is utilized for seeing the full visual of the world) and beginning to pretend it has limitations. So be very gentle and very careful with the baby in the first few weeks after birth as many of the adjustments to those limitations are made in the very tips of the baby's fingers at that time.

By the way, for those of you who have the audacity to put little mittens on your newborn child, please know that this is most uncomfortable for babies. You may think you are protecting them from scratching and harming themselves. However, if you would converse with them instead, the likelihood is you wouldn't have to put those boxing gloves on them, and they could have their hands free. Just take their tiny little wrists and hold their hands up to your face and converse with them. Let them touch you. And Dads, please shave, and get close enough so that they can inhale you.

Young children do need that physical contact of the human being, especially of the mother and father. You know the reason they like to be held close to your heart, don't you? This is so they can feel the heart go *thump, thump, thump*—the same rhythmic sound they heard within the light process. As they come closer to Earth, they begin to hear the same sound and feel the rhythms of Earth, for it is the same rhythm as the heartbeat of the human world. Mother Earth has her own heartbeat, the human has its own heartbeat, and that is why the child is so secure when it is at the mother's breast.

I know that many of you are thinking, "No, no. The child is so secure simply because it was in the mother's belly hearing her heartbeat all that time." That is truth. But it is also truth that in the light where the child's spiritual light essence existed prior to entering into the birth process, that same identical sound was there. What is that sound? It is the sound of the evolutionary Earth. It is a sound unheard on any other planet in existence. For instance, if you were to go to the world of Sirius, the heartbeat there would be somewhere between fourteen to fifteen times faster than that of the human heartbeat. Sirius works at that vibration and yours works at what you hear it now to be.

Year 2. As you move into the second year of your life, you become much more aware of the duality presence of Earth. You realize that "up" has a "down" because you fall through space more often than not. Unless someone is holding onto you a lot at first, those little rubber legs of yours just turn into mush and down you go again.

Now, here is something fascinating to share. I cannot imagine anyone about to have a baby not wanting a copy of these words, so please listen to what I am saying. In your second year, you are also beginning to establish your communication skills with the Earth plane. You will find throughout your first year and into the second that you are developing your "eye conversations." In other words, in your attempts to get others to communicate with you, you develop a way of speaking through your eyes.

At that age, you discover that human adults are not very cooperative because they are operating within their full ego veils, whereas yours are still at a very thin, light vibration. Your communicative skills are beginning to develop and you are eager to enter into conversation with your parents. If your parents cannot understand your eye conversations, you start using your voice. If, for example, your parents listened closely, they would hear you saying such things as, "The perimeter of your Earth has shrunken to somewhat near a 'diasadidal' moment of time and space. So if you would pay attention to me, we could probably…" Meanwhile, your parents are intent on getting you to say, "Mama, Dada." This should make you rather frustrated, don't you think? And your parents wonder why you cry! Well, if you think about it, that would be a pretty good reason to cry.

As you establish contact with the human world in your second year, the veils of your ego also begin to strengthen and become more intense. You know that you cannot do the astral traveling as you did before and this intensifies the adjustment. That is, unless you have a father or mother who knows about metaphysics and teaches you how to get out, which is of course to their advantage as well.

Year 3. We move along rapidly into the third year, when you understand that the human world is not what you expected it to be. You came here with strong intentions to really learn the human process completely this time. You were determined to remember that you are first and foremost *spirit*. Now, suddenly, all of the memories are fading.

At age three, you are starting to lock into your physical presence. By now you are expected to walk fully on two legs. Well, because you had forgotten about this thing called *gravity*, you fall down a lot. You also fall down a lot because you have forgotten that you can fly and that you can disperse your molecular structure. At the same time, you know that you could walk across the floor twenty-five times if you wanted to, but why bother? Your parents still carry you a lot, and it works out better that way. Oh, yes, you are quite smart at three years, don't you know?

Now listen to me carefully. Most of you in this gathering are metaphysicians, yes? Most of you are learning how to communicate without using spoken words, and most of you are finding out when you communicate this way, you get more of what you want, yes? This is truth. If you look into another's eyes deeply enough, you know the other person can understand what you are saying. Well, this is what a three-year-old child is still trying to do. It is communicating with you on other levels, but you, the human adults, are trying to define your child's reality. Instead of letting them define their own reality, you are defining it for them; that is, until they get up to the beautiful age of four.

Year 4. At four, you want to define your own reality. With still a faint memory of where you came from and clear ideas of what this Earth plane is really all about, your parents have to hang on for dear life at this stage.

At about the fourth year, you begin to talk about your friend that lives under the bed. I know most of you were told by adults, "You stop that; otherwise, they are going to put you in a padded room and throw away the key, and you won't be able to come out anymore. And if you go to school and talk like that in front of your teachers, they are going to think Mommy and Daddy have raised a crazy person. Don't talk about your friend under the bed to anyone. In fact, don't even tell me about your imaginary friend." So you just pretend they don't exist.

Year 5. When you grow into the beauty of the fifth year, the whole world begins to shake. In this year, you enter the mesmerizing school system of pre-schools and kindergartens where you make new friends. You have found all of these new friends, who, by the way, are all just as trapped in bodies as you are. You sit about talking with them, and you say to the one sitting at the next desk—not even using your voices quite yet, "Are we really stuck over here?" Your friend replies, "Yes, we are. I have been trying to get out of here for five years, but I can't find my way out." And it goes on like that, back and forth amongst all the children in the classroom. Meanwhile, the teacher is saying "A, B, C, D, E..." and you are thinking, "Well, how is it that she still has not learned the alphabet?" Yes, what you have to go through as a child is often trying, isn't it?

Year 6. We now fast forward to the age of six because at that age you master the Earth plane. At six, you realize you no longer need adults in your world. Since they don't know the first thing about your life, you decide not to have anything to do with them. Instead, you end up moping a lot, just sitting around and pondering life. You look at the world you came from and where you can't wait to return to. Meanwhile, they are telling you, "Grow up and stop acting like a child." Oh, gracious, that is such a horrible thing to say to a child.

Year 7. Moving into that final year, the seventh year, of the unfolding blueprint is one of the most exciting times. The seventh year is the year of transition. Most importantly, this is the year when you fully enact the ego system as you transition from the seventh into the eighth year. Some children will advance rapidly while others will move at a slower pace, but sometime within that year, the veils are fully enacted. And for this reason, children at this age become almost impossible to deal with. I know most parents of seven-year-olds would agree with that. I also know that parents of fourteen-year-olds might want to disagree because they know that fourteen is also an age of absolute insanity for parents. Perhaps it would help to remember that a major reconstruction of the blueprint takes place every seven years.

Re-Setting the Blueprint in the First Seven Years

Let's talk now in general terms about the first seven years of the blueprint. As I have already said, many of the patterns that affect the rest of your life are established in this time period. Within those first seven years, you set the energies that you are going to experience in this lifetime. Again, this is assuming that all the life plans of your blueprint are going just the way you set them when you were still in the Creator's Light.

What happens when the parents you picked change plans on you a little bit? You simply try to re-set your original plans, or for lack of better words, you become a bit intolerant. That is to say, you have become aware once again of certain rules and regulations in the Third Dimension that you had forgotten. Nevertheless, you still try, even insistently at times, to return to your original blueprint. In most cases, you have to adjust parts of your blueprint, and sometimes, re-set the entire plan.

There is another scenario that may occur, and that is when the set of parents you picked completely lose track of their ability to interact with the Creator. Let's suppose they use physical force to train you to do things the way *they* think things should be done. This automatically requires that you reset your blueprint once more.

Please follow what I am saying here: You come with an established blueprint, a blueprint that was all set and ready to go before your birth. But if your parents act in ways incongruent with light and love itself, and they begin to do harmful things to you, the child, you immediately re-set the blueprint to establish new and certain safe zones for yourself. Thus, in those first seven years, my friends, the blueprint often needs to be worked and reworked, much of it due to the parenting of those you have been charged to.

In such cases, you can establish within the blueprint anytime in the first seven years what is called a "matriarchal matrix." The matriarchal matrix will encase your light and prevent you from experiencing any form of physical punishment. So if you are being physically abused, you can set this energy about yourself and it will protect you until you can break free of the abuse. However, any effects from abuse will affect your blueprint throughout your life. In truth, many of you will not begin to re-establish your blueprint until you are thirty or forty years old, which is when you begin the healing process.

I may be repeating myself here, but I want you to understand that the blueprint which you establish in the first seven years may not get changed until you have gone through five or six cycles of seven-year transitions, or until you are around thirty-six years or forty-two years of age. At that age, you begin to see where the blueprint needs to be adjusted and you usually begin some form of healing. You begin to re-establish your life and do the things that will vibrate to that focus, often making it appear that much of your life is amiss. Until such time, you live the vast majority of your life based on the blueprint that was—forgive this, but for impact's sake— hammered into you.

As I speak, I can feel the energy of some of you. You may not feel it, but some of you are almost going into a fetal position, so to speak. Some of you are pulling your energy back because you recall that yours was not as beautiful a childhood as you had planned on. Yet, try to understand that what ends up happening is not always what you put in for. Still, your blueprint can be changed. Again, this requires a form of healing that takes place only when you have activated within your cellular memory what is called the "chromosomes of defense" systems. Then as you seek to understand how your blueprint got adjusted in those first years of life, the healing process begins to work at a new level of awareness.

How many of you can attribute your life to something that happened when you were three years old? Most of you cannot; most of you will not. But believe me, if I were to take a poll of the audience tonight, many of you would definitely be part of those who experienced something which was not planned for in your first three years of life. You say, "Wait a minute, Kirael. Are you in any way suggesting that many of us were beaten up or abused as children?"

My friends, you cannot begin to understand what abuse is until you are the child in the situation. You cannot begin to understand what it means when Mommy has had a bad day. First, you know that you are in love—purely, fully in love—and Mommy is coming home after picking you up from the babysitter. She has worked all day, and she brings you home and puts you down in this "cage." You know what that looks like, right? It is called a crib. She puts you in this cage, throws a bunch of stuffed animals on top of you, and says, "There, play. I'm going to go fix dinner." And you say things like, "Excuse me. Didn't Master Kirael say we are supposed to interact right here? Aren't we supposed to be rubbing faces and things like that? Master Kirael! Master Kirael! Master Kirael!" I come over there and I say, "What do you want, little one?" And you say, "Mom is not doing it." Then I say, "Well, there is not much I can do until she calls me."

Do you see what I am saying? This becomes abuse of the child. You say, "Kirael, I can't be with them every moment of their day." I guess if you can't, you can't. Nevertheless, do you see what I am saying? Abuse is not necessarily about being struck with an open hand. Abuse is, in my humble opinion, about not being present with that child as it grows, but instead forcing the child to set its experiences into the blueprint alone. For instance, that little child who just got popped in the crib cage with a bunch of furry stuffed animals studies how this relates to the blueprint. It begins to record its experiences by the way Mom and Dad are acting, thinking this must be how it works on the Earth plane. So it begins to set its blueprint based on what Mom and Dad are doing. You might say that Mom and Dad's extremely loud conversation in the other room can't bother a two-year-old. Trust me, my friends. Children are more affected than you could ever imagine. This is where the real abuse is.

You say, "Well, Kirael, people who have been abused physically or sexually or mentally, or whatever, would disagree with you." And I understand that, but I am talking to the vast majority of you out there. There are many levels of abuse, and each and every one of you has experienced being abused on one level or another. You just didn't recognize it as such. When Mom turned to you and said, "I have had a busy day. Now shut up!" that hurts deeply, my friends. It hurts very deeply.

Most of you are not able to remember these moments because when they happened, you would say, "Oh, I don't like that. I'll just pull back, out of the way, where I don't have to deal with it." Then you would wait for Mom or Dad to calm down and love you again. However, that interim in which you did not feel their love is registered in your blueprint.

Therefore, you learn at a very early age how not to love all the time. It is conditional love. You learn it. The conditions are set based upon your actions; therefore, you set your conditions of love based on the actions of the people that you interact with. Oh yes, my friends, you do. You say, "But Kirael, I don't know if *abuse* is the right word. I think it's too strong." I don't, my friends. I truly don't. Those first seven years when you are establishing the blueprint for life is such an important time. It is such a dramatic time.

"But wait, Master Kirael, what if we made a mistake? What if we didn't mean to yell, but we did." Well, go apologize, for God's sake. By going to your baby and tickling their belly and squeezing them until they giggle doesn't mean that everything is all right again. You truly need to explain to these little ones what just happened. You can say things like, "Mom and Dad are complete blithering idiots sometimes, and that is why we are arguing with each other," or you can tell the real truth. You can say, "Mom and Dad haven't learned how to be in love yet, so what we do is we take out that lack of learning on each other, and we raise our voices. And because we haven't learned how to really fully communicate yet"—you are telling this to a two-year-old, by the way—"we escalate things until we can get a certain sense of fulfillment from it."

Of course, the little one is going to understand that, isn't it? Perhaps the words, no, but the feeling, yes. You see, when the words come from love, a baby understands them, because babies know only love. And when there is a lack of love, the child learns very quickly to readjust the blueprint. Hence, through the first seven years, the blueprint will be adjusted over and over again, layer upon layer upon layer. Finally, the child learns everything that you can teach it, and then the awareness becomes, "I am seven years old. I get to start a new life," and it does.

I could talk endlessly on this subject, but for now I would prefer that we open to your questions. Therefore, if you have questions, we can talk about anything along these lines. You can also ask personal questions if you must, but please keep them on this evening's subject. For instance, if you had a traumatic situation happen when you were of the age of five or six or seven, and you are just beginning to remember it and you want to talk about it tonight, let's talk about it. We will place very few limits on your questions this evening.

Questions & Answers

Traveling Companions in the Womb

Good evening, Master Kirael. I do a type of healing work that involves emotional clearing, often taking the patient back to a time in utero. I have found that it is a very common perception that there was a twin, or companion, or sometimes even two or three others with the patient in utero. Often the perceived loss of that companion at birth is very traumatic, resulting in feelings of guilt and failure although it could have been the process of the survival of the fittest. I would love for to you expand on this.

KIRAEL: When your patients return to their time in utero, they recognize that at that time they were still traveling a lot with the angelic world. Most people are aware of the "escort angel" that comes to take them back home to the Creator Light. Most are not familiar, though, with what I would term their "arrival angel." Arrival angels are the ones who accompany you to the Earth plane. Actually, sometimes even multiples of angels will travel with you, depending on your status as you leave the Light Beingness. So what is commonly being experienced by your patients is not another physical life in utero but more along the lines of an angel or of a brother or sister from their soul family. You see, when you release the limits of the human flesh or the human body presence, you begin to realize that you have access to all levels of awareness.

For instance, when you decided that you were coming onto the Earth plane, maybe you were a little bit nervous about it. So you said to some of your brothers and sisters of the same soul family, "Would you go along with me?" Yes, some agreed to come here with you, but not necessarily to enter the womb with you. Meaning they agreed to always be with you in some fashion or another while you were in the womb.

So the *separation anxiety*, as they call it, or the feeling that you must overcome, is a term that you learned in the 10% mind. But when you do come through the birthing channel, you are automatically releasing the energies of a brother or sister from your soul family, or of your arrival angel or whatever else it might be. And as you release them, you feel a sense of separation from them.

Segmented Chromosomes

In your opening statement you talked about how the blueprint is altered with abuse. You also said something about the chromosomes of defense. Could you elaborate on these chromosomes?

KIRAEL: Each of you has certain segmented chromosomes within each system. In fact, your doctor world and your science world are about to explode with all of these new awakenings. For instance, they know that a chromosome exists within you which will actually affect how long you will live. It does not indicate a year but a more general timeframe in which a person lives. Let's say that part of your blueprint is to experience very old age, so the blueprint will infuse this chromosome of youth and vitality to operate extensively until that time.

There is also a chromosome set at a certain vibration to allow your defense modalities to activate at a certain rate. For example, if you are one of those people who become defensive at almost everything, it means that your blueprint is set within that chromosomal sector at a higher vibration. It also means that your anger peaks at a much quicker rate, making you easily agitated or more difficult to get along with.

Almost every chromosome in your body is what we call a "segmented chromosome." Each is locked in within the DNA process itself. Each and every one of these chromosomes has a specific part of the blueprint implemented into it. That is how you move the blueprint through the system.

Memory Chromosomes

I remember that as a little girl I used to love to lie on my bed and look out the window at the sky, just daydreaming and watching the clouds float by. Sometimes I would feel a sense of sadness. My question is: As children grow up and the veils solidify around them, are they consciously aware of losing touch? Or do children experience it as a passing, nostalgic feeling of sadness?

KIRAEL: Within your blueprint, you have memory chromosomes which hold the events of the first seven years of your life. These memories lock into the blueprint certain things that you want to be aware of throughout life. So when you lay on the bed looking out the window and felt a certain sadness, it was literally to remind you that "out there" is where everything really is, and "in here" is what you have established as part of your blueprint to experience the life journey on Earth.

The "Boogie Man" is Part of the Blueprint

I have a strong memory of dreams when I was very young; some of them were really, really wonderful dreams. Then there was one recurring dream of a "boogie man." I think I was maybe five or six years old, and I remember it being up in the corner of my room. Why?

KIRAEL: Why? I will tell you why. The "boogie man" you call it?

Yes, it was just up there and it had that looming, boogie man presence.

KIRAEL: I will answer it the best I can, my friend. It is not just in your case, but in many cases the blueprint calls for a life that is charmed. And written in those kinds of blueprints are what you might call "the good guys and the bad guys," the "angels and the dark forces," and so on. As a rule, these are figments of your reality force of imagination. I said "reality force of imagination" because you can align these into your blueprint to remind you every now and then that the perfect, charmed life that you have established is going to have a few glitches in it along the way. Now, you are not supposed to remember them for as long as you do, but being human, the possibility exists that you will.

By the way, I have met your little friend. Let me just say this much about him: Not only was he not a boogie man; he was a full-fledged angel acting out a part that you put in your blueprint. One day he will return to you when you are back on the other side, and he will say, "You owe me for that one." The truth is the truth.

Nightmares are Actually Blueprint Lessons

Before asking my question, I want first to unload a little emotion. I am looking at this from a child's perspective, but also from being a parent of four. In terms of the way I parented, now that I am more awakened, I have come to the realization that I could certainly have done some things differently with my children, and I have tried to let go of some of that guilt. I have also reconnected with my children and given them unconditional love. It is one of the things that makes me happy when I think of the success I have had in raising my children.

My question is about nightmares. When you were talking about the colicky baby, it made me remember my daughter who used to have nightmares when she was very, very young. I was wondering why I didn't feel it was anything drastic for a very young child to have nightmares.

KIRAEL: Let me answer that one for you because it is a fabulous question and because the answer is partly found in the blueprint. Within the blueprint is found memories of other worlds, other places, other things. Oftentimes children at a very young age will tap into other lifetimes that are registered in the blueprint. These may have been traumatic experiences in previous lifetimes which appear as nightmares. A nightmare is really the replaying of the experience to be able to know where to put it in the blueprint and in the cellular consciousness so that it can be replayed at a later time in life. Does that make sense?

Not exactly, but...

KIRAEL: Let me try again. Understand that in the blueprint, my friend, are many of the things that you are going to work on in this lifetime. Some of these things include horrendous acts from other lifetimes that you are going to need to deal with in this lifetime. Therefore, while you are establishing the blueprint in the first seven years, you are actually getting visuals of those old acts. In this manner, you can know where to place them in the current blueprint, as well as where to imbed them in the cellular consciousness. You can also decide the appropriate time to deal with each experience.

Then why don't we all have nightmares? Not all of my children seemed to have these kinds of dreams when they were young.

KIRAEL: It depends on what situations from previous lifetimes each child has decided to bring along with them into this lifetime. Younger souls will bring in many more of these situations. Older souls will usually have taken care of all of these processes by now and will have come here for other reasons, which is neither a good nor a bad thing.

Choosing to Be Born Prematurely

About a month ago, I had a healing in which I was working on my issues of self-worth. In that healing it was brought forth that these issues started for me in the womb. When I asked why, the answer was because my mother was in an emotional state at that time due to a death in the family and that this was literally "brain-zapping" some of my energy. Hence, it is my understanding that I literally chose at that point to be born at seven months instead of at the usual nine. How did this choice in the womb affect the blueprint of my life or of other individuals who go through similar trauma?

KIRAEL: Dramatically. Quite dramatically. The reason I say this is because you were a couple of months premature, weren't you?

I was born at seven months.

KIRAEL: At seven months you made it through the transitional stage of the pregnancy. This has a dramatic implication because you might have been affected by your mother's going through a family death experience. You will have learned from that memory; thus, it is something you will not have to experience in this lifetime. This is why you have memory of the death, so that you can adjust your blueprint and throughout your entire life not have a great fear of death. And you will have set the blueprint in that manner.

As for those of you born in a premature state, understand this: There is a certain magic to each and every one of you, and the magic is that you have cut one plan short so that you may extend another plan. The shortage of the blueprint in the womb is extended in the human world in the first year. What that normally means is you wind up living over here for an extremely long time, which is how you adjust the blueprint.

The Benefits of Being Born Late

What happens to a child that is born later than its expected birth date?

KIRAEL: We refer to them as cowards. No, I am just having fun! [*laughter*]

That is a very interesting question, and I will tell you why: Those that are born late, after the usual nine months, usually end up coming out through a cesarean birth, right? The technology now allows for babies to be born soon after their expected due date. But back in the 1400's and 1500's, babies could go sometimes a full month beyond and be born even in the tenth month. That would totally reset the blueprint.

You see, the blueprint is usually set for nine months before birth, right? When you go beyond that more than three or four days, you have to re-set the blueprint. It usually turns out very well, however, because you hold onto some segments of the original blueprint and refocus new energy into the new blueprint, and you end up with a combination blueprint. The result is that the individual often ends up being a borderline genius due to the dual-blueprint faction going on. Did this happen to you?

Yes.

KIRAEL: That is what happens quite often. The interesting part is that you will either be a genius more in the first half or in the last half of your life.

So if, for whatever reason, you don't consider yourself a genius right now, do have all of the fun and merriment you want to have. Enjoy it all until about your forty-second year, at which point the second of your two blueprints will kick in. Meaning, a new set of chromosomes will emerge, and you will begin to have visions of things you never thought possible. You will be able to do calculus—well, maybe not quite that dramatic, but darn near that dramatic—because the second blueprint that has been lying dormant until then will burst forth in freedom for you.

The Aunt is the Mother in the Blueprint

I have a niece and a nephew who are very different from one another. They were raised in very different kinds of environments in their first two years of life. My parents, my sister, and I are acting somewhat as their parents and we see such big differences in their personalities and interactions. How much did their environments affect them at that age?

KIRAEL: There is a woman seated in the first row here tonight who was supposed to have a child born to her, but when it didn't work out, the child ended up being born to another woman. It may seem unbelievable that these things can happen, but it is possible.

In your case, let's talk about the little girl first. She was the first one born, wasn't she? Well, this little girl could very likely have waited for you, but she was in a hurry, so she chose your sister to be born through. In that way she knew she could be close to you. I can tell you this: Your interactions with this little girl influence and adjust her blueprint more than her interactions with her mother do. Her younger brother, on the other hand, was a designated energy of the mother. So a totally different set of blueprints have been in alignment for him as it relates to his mother.

In general, blueprints are adjusted again at the time of birth through vibrational frequencies. They are then set into the chromosomes so they can interact with whomever they are working with. Naturally, the parents, especially the mothers, have certain defined effects on a child's blueprint. In the case of your little niece, however, the major effect came through you because her blueprint is so closely aligned with your blueprint, and that will never change for as long as you or she stays on the Earth plane. There will be a camaraderie that will grow between you which you will probably understand only on a level of the blueprint itself.

Isn't your sister your twin? We could make that the entire topic for another evening, couldn't we?

Premature Babies and New Technology

Because of advanced technology these days, most babies born prematurely at six months or earlier can survive. This couldn't have happened thirty or forty years ago. What besides new technology is the difference between now and then?

KIRAEL: If babies are born before the sixth month, it is possible that the conditions within the mother's womb or the nurturing agents within the physical body may not align with the blueprint. In such cases, the child will try to establish a different set of blueprints, one they would have gotten as they traveled back and forth between the worlds during their time in the womb.

The premature baby will also make some sort of contact with another member of its soul family. There will often be an exchange of energies from the soul family to assist in the resetting of the blueprint. The other member will bring in a new blueprint and help to establish it. And that is why there have been many difficulties in the past with premature births. Hopefully that will change now with the advances in technology.

When a Mother Dies During Childbirth

What happens in situations where the mother dies during childbirth?

KIRAEL: As a rule, it is part of the overall program. Normally the child coming in will be aware that the mother is planning to exit at that point. Therefore, the blueprint will be adjusted to allow another to fill the role of mother. The child will usually try to attach their blueprint to someone who was close to the mother, looking for the person who will fill his or her needs the best.

Exit Plans in the Blueprint

I was wondering about exit plans in the blueprint. I am not quite sure exactly when, but somewhere between the age of one and seven, my father dove into a swimming pool and pulled my body from the bottom of the pool. I am assuming that was an exit plan that I perhaps didn't take advantage of.

KIRAEL: It was a nice try, though. You deserve great credit for trying, but you didn't get away with it. You must be aware that at one time you were kin to one of the queen dolphins of this universe. What a large mistake that was, trying to dive into water to find a way of exit! You could have lain down at the bottom of the pool for four hours, and your dad could have walked down and picked you up later. There was no way that an exit could have happened. It just wasn't going to work.

My theory is that you decided you would test the waters. That is not a play on words. You decided you would test the waters to see if you could transcend levels, and you knew it really couldn't go on because it is not in your blueprint to get out, right? So that is why you took the little tumbler into the swimming pool and just lay down there on the bottom for a little bit just to see how close you could come to the experience. And have you not lived most of your life pretty much the same way—just to see how close you can come to the fullness of experiences?

Are exit plans programmed into the blueprint?

KIRAEL: Oftentimes, yes. Well, there is always an exit programmed into the blueprint, and it is malleable, meaning it can be moved around in the blueprint. If you came to a stage in life where you no longer wanted to exist in this light, you could take on some sort of disease as your exit route. Whether you actually went that route would depend on the programming of your chromosome of in-lightenment. This chromosome allows you to utilize the exit plan, but it is located so far below all the other chromosomes in your blueprint that you normally find a way to continue on with your life.

Healing Childhood Abuse

While you were speaking about physical abuse, I started having many kinds of sensations, especially physical sensations. How do we heal abuse on all four subtle bodies? I want to heal myself so that I may assist others.

KIRAEL: Beautiful question, my friend. First, I would ask that you work diligently with your Unseen Self, or higher self. Second, I would suggest that you begin healing others on a regular basis. In healing others you will allow your 90% mind to download more of the blueprint into your 10%, where you can begin to address and heal the abuses that were suffered. The memory chromosomes, which I spoke of just a moment ago, will begin to awaken as you heal others. As you heal others, you will also awaken the love that you have suppressed all these years.

My question has to do with my children's blueprints and how they were reconfigured by the abuse they experienced growing up. Now as adults entering into their thirties, what would help them to heal?

KIRAEL: A copy of this work would go a long way in helping them to heal. I am very serious; most people don't realize that abuse can take place on many different levels. Then, by learning that their blueprint is still being worked through, as is yours, they can re-establish their original blueprints. Hopefully, what they learn can help *their* own children establish their blueprints in a different manner.

Karma-Proof Moments in Childhood

Children in the first few years are so truthful, sometimes brutally truthful, especially to each other. I was wondering whether they create more karma amongst themselves or whether they resolve a lot of karma at that age because of their truthfulness.

KIRAEL: That is a fabulous question, and you will probably find the answer just a wee bit surprising because very little karma is established in the first seven years. The blueprint is already filled with karma from other lifetimes, along with other experiences and plans that you have for this lifetime. So when you get into a bit of a shouting match with one of your fellow young ones, the honesty and the truth that emanate from those disagreements is oftentimes, let's say, "karma-proof." Because they are so honest, what they say is not really meant to hurt another. What they say may hurt right there on the spot, so to speak, which may also lead to some pushing and shoving and the like. However, these incidents are normally not written into the blueprint. We would consider them more as interactions with an Earth plane that one isn't fully familiar with yet, and the outcome is almost always a potential healing.

Have you ever noticed how children are so forgiving? This is because they are based in so much truth in those first seven years. Children are so brutally honest in most cases that it is not an exception, but the rule. So when karma is established at this young age, it is usually insignificant and easily healed.

Guaranteed Karma for Kids AND Parents

What about teasing, which is looked upon as normal children's behavior around the ages of five and six? When children tease each other a lot, doesn't that incur karma?

KIRAEL: As I said earlier, if it is just a case of light teasing with words, there is no karma.

But parents, hang on. If the parental figure continually encourages their kids to tease and fight, the kids as well as the parents incur karma. In order for that to happen, you have to affect the 10% brain to activate the chromosomes within the system to open up a karmic issue. So parents who would influence their children by saying, "Good job, Johnny, I'm glad you punched him in the nose," will find themselves helping their child incur some karma. And remember, the parents, too, are picking up some karma of their own.

Too Much TV Triggers "Star Sitters"

You spoke earlier about how children's blueprints are reset in the first seven years by the influence of the parents. Now there is talk about a third "parent"—the media as a babysitter for many children. In the last few years, the time children spend watching TV and playing computer video games has increased dramatically. Would you address the effects on children, especially in the early years, from all the violence that they see on TV and in computer games?

KIRAEL: Yes, I will not only talk about it, I will probably shock half the world with this one. Within the blueprint are "star sitters." Star sitters are activator points in the blueprint that can be adjusted by outside influences. It would be highly improbable that these star sitters are activated in the blueprint of a normal child growing up. But if they are constantly being bombarded with the influx of outer influences, the star sitters will begin to refocus the blueprint.

When this happens the blueprint is thrown out of alignment with the 10% mind and the 90% mind is more highly activated. This might actually be a good thing except that it makes it difficult for the human to live in a world of 10% thinking. People will find themselves in a bit of a bind, so to speak, because as the star sitters are activated, they actually careen particles of light off of each other until they begin to vibrate to such a degree that the blueprint is now subjected to these outside forces.

The end result is the persons, or children in this case, will seek more of this stimuli. You will find many of these individuals eventually working in the world of computers in some fashion or another because they need more and more stimulus to keep themselves going. The chromosomes that have been affected by the activated star sitters are now feeding energy back through the system at a rate that a normal brain cannot tolerate. Therefore, the brain has to be in a constant state of expansion, and the spiral continues ad infinitum.

Does this activation just expand the 90% consciousness or could it result in such things as attention deficit disorders and hyperactivity?

KIRAEL: When an expansion of the 90% mind takes place, the 90% awareness is downloading information into the 10% mind without your request. For instance, when you meditate you are requesting input from the 90% awareness and you select what you want of the 90%. However, when a child is constantly bombarded with external stimuli, it causes the 90% to expand, thereby forcing its energy into the 10%. The outcome is often that a child is then diagnosed as having attention deficit type disorders.

Therefore, is a child's physical body not ready to deal with all the brain expansion?

KIRAEL: That is correct. The child cannot keep up with the brain expansions, especially when it is going through new phases of growth. This is why certain children will have sudden outbursts of emotions. Here again is a subject that we could spend an entire evening discussing. [See *Kirael Shift Report*, June 2000 on video games and children of the Shift for more information.]

The Blueprints of Shift Babies

The medium, Rev. Sterling, talked about the blueprints of the third-dimensional matrix in your book, "Kirael Volume II: The Genesis Matrix (Chapter 8)." There he said that frequency adjustments to this planet's mainframe systemic converters would be made just before the Shift. I was wondering if you could tell us how these frequency adjustments will affect the children coming onto the Earth plane at that time, particularly the one-to seven-year-olds.

KIRAEL: Those children are already being pre-programmed, if you will. Their matrix light is being pre-programmed within their blueprints to adjust to the new energy forces at the time of the Shift. In fact, a filtration system located just outside of your matrix has been designed to help them process the incoming energy at that time. You see, they will not be caught off guard at the time of the Shift.

Since about 1987, the children are coming onto the Earth plane with a greater awareness of the Shift already set in their blueprints and are therefore better prepared. They are being rewarded in that all this is to take place in their lifetime. The ones being born currently and hereafter have pre-programmed their light to align into this awareness. So the factors which we talk about in this book will make more sense to a six-year-old than to a forty-six-year-old.

Activation of the Blueprint Before the Shift

Could you explain more about how to maximize returning to our cellular consciousness from this blueprint? It sounds like the blueprint is more of a block that we have put on the cellular consciousness. But is there some way we can reactivate our cellular consciousness by reverting back to the original blueprint? Or do we need to find a new mechanism to work with the blueprint as the Shift approaches?

KIRAEL: That is a beautiful question, my friend. Let me clarify just a couple of the points that you made so that they might vibrate a little bit better in your thought processes.

It is not as though you have put some form of blockage between the blueprint and the cellular consciousness. The elements of the blueprint are actually, shall we say, "inter-faced" in the cellular consciousness itself. So, when the blueprint is amplified through what we call a "serrate energy," various elements of the blueprint leak from the 90% portion of your awareness into the 10% portion. At this point, you place words to what is taking place. In fact, you start bringing all the words you hear out of the 90%, which you then formulate into the context of your life journey.

Each part of the cellular consciousness absorbs segments of the blueprint which are to be utilized at a future time. It is set up in such fashion that the 90% mind knows when to begin interaction with the blueprint. The 90% knows how to refocus the blueprint so that it will settle into the areas where it is supposed to be. The 10% mind, the learned part of your journey here, begins to reset the blueprint out of fear, and out of what we consider to be the ego system. So the plan, as you are asking about it, has been established.

I am glad you asked this question as it relates to the Shift because it might be the most important answer I give all night. As you arrive at this thing called the Shift, everyone's blueprint will begin to emerge from the 90% awareness, which means the 90% part of the mind will begin to segment itself, and it will search out all of those layers that have been superimposed into the conscious parts of the body. Then it will begin to draw them back into the memory banks of the 10% awareness. Therefore, eventually, as you close in on what we call the Shift, you will begin to see patterns of energy that will literally explode in your 10% mind. You will begin to attain great insights into your past lives as well as into parts of this life. Much of the blueprint that you have stored away will become available to you as the Shift of Earth unfolds.

Chromosomes of Change

You have talked a lot this evening about different kinds of chromosomes found within a blueprint. Right now I am in a period of change, so can I call on the chromosomes of change to start a new career? Is that how it works?

KIRAEL: Oh, I would say you are about to be born free! In all sincerity, my friend, yes, call on them. Normally the physical body has a whole "gaggle" of chromosomes of change, as I like to say. You can call on these chromosomes to establish what you want to do and how you want to do it. And through the practice of the Four Pillars of Conscious Creation—your masterminds, your sleepstate programming, your prayers and meditations, you will know exactly how to create a new, "born-free" life.

Closing Statement

I believe we have pretty much come to the end of our time together this evening. Hopefully, you have found it a bit on the fun side, and hopefully, it has also been enlightening. I know that your angels and the guides are thrilled with your own evolution by the questions you asked this evening. My friends, one day you will learn it isn't about whether or not you come to see me; it is about you coming to see *you*. And that is your truth.

Good evening, my friends.

4 Healing Karma

Opening Statement

KIRAEL: Good evening.

We come here this evening to talk about *karma*. Now, karma can come through many different religious or spiritualist voices. There is the Hindu version of karma. There is the Buddhist version of karma. There are even references to karma in your Holy Bible; they just don't use the word. Instead, they simply say such things as, "Whatever seeds you sow, so shall you reap." This is mentioned not just once but a number of times in the Good Book.

The truth, my friends, is that over many years, karma has often been equated to being a very bad thing. But believe me, you live in a world that is based solely in duality. If it is so based in duality, then for every bit of good karma you create, you must be careful of the other side of it. Conversely, if you create a bunch of bad karma, you have the right to create a bunch on the good as well.

You see, karma is a beautiful thing, and I want you to be very clear on this because the world oftentimes mistakenly believes that karma equates to fate. Fate is an entirely different reality. Sometimes you think that karma is faith, when it has little to do with your faith. Let me explain by taking you back into a time and space where time didn't exist. I will take you back into a lighted arena when you were nothing more, nothing less, than the beautiful energy pattern of your Creator's Light, waiting to incarnate on the Earth plane.

First, let me make something perfectly clear to you, my friends: You don't just pop over here to the Earth every time you get this little urge. You just don't say, "Excuse me, God, I'd like to go over there to the Earth plane and do a couple of lives because I am a few short on lifetimes." You can't do that. In fact, I will be honest with you, my friends. The light of truth is that you have to wait awhile before you can get over here because there are many different reality focuses you need to abide by to qualify for incarnation.

Life in the Movies: A Metaphor

We are going to use the metaphor of a movie theater experience this evening to illustrate how you arrive here on the Earth plane. Pick out in your mind the very best movie that you have seen recently. Was there a chance that you had to wait in line to get there? And when you were waiting in line, weren't you excited? Well, there are also times when you are waiting in line and you become a bit afraid. What of? Well, a guy standing in front of you says to his girlfriend, "Oh, I love this movie! It's my third time. You should see when the car with the star in it flies off the cliff and sprays all over the ocean floor." You think, "Well, I might as well get out of line. I don't need to see the movie now if I already know how it comes out."

Let's assume that you decide to stay in line and they finally open the doors. The first thing you do is go to the ticket-taker man who says to you, "Do you have your ticket to get in?" Well, of course you do. If you did all the things you should have done, you have got your wee ticket, you give it to the ticket man, and he says, "Please, go to that space over there, and the usher will show you through."

The first thing you want to do is go in, but you've got to get your popping-corns and your sodas and things like that. So you go to a big display, and you pick out all the things that you want. Someone behind the counter says, "You realize now that there's a price you've got to pay for all this." And you say to him, "You're right!" In truth, the cost doesn't matter because you are determined. Next, the usher seats you in this nice soft-cushioned chair. The movie lights switch on and there you are in the movie, just enjoying it. Then, all too soon, the darn movie comes to an end, and you leave the theater in search of a new adventure.

Do you understand the metaphor here? When you are in this place called the Creator's Light, you want to come to the movies. And now I have to tell you something, my friends: The Earth plane is one of the most fabulous movies that you have ever created. This is one grand movie. There you are standing in line, and the first thing you do is go over to the ticket takers—your angel friends. They say, "All right. So you got permission to come to Earth and do all the things you want to do. Is that right?" And you say, "Yes, I'm ready to go." And the ticket taker says, "Let me see your ticket." And you hold up your light pass and you say, "I have earned my rights." And the angels let you in and send you to the display counter where you finalize the details for your movie experience.

At the counter, you say, "Here are my program potentials. I want my programs perfectly established now. I am going to Earth and I want to do a certain number of things there. You see, I've been over there a number of times. Right now I remember everything really clearly, but I know when I get there, my memory will fade. So I want to be extremely clear now on what I will do in the movies on the Earth plane. Here are my plans." And you list down all of the beautiful things you plan to experience.

Now you might ask, "Kirael, am I committed to that program? Can I change it in any way?" These are just your desires, my friends. They are what you are desirous of doing. So then the guidance energies behind the counter say, "All right. Reach down and pick out what you want." And you say, "I'll take that mom and dad," instead of popcorn and soda, or whatever you want. The programs are then all established, and off you go, and you sit in the balcony area. While waiting for the movie to start, you know there are these things they call commercials and previews of coming attractions—that would equate to being in Mom's womb. All of a sudden, the screen erupts in sights and sounds. The first thing you see is that big lion on the big screen. And he roars his "RRROARRR," scaring you half to death—bad choice of words—scaring you half to life. Yet the excitement far outweighs the fear, and the movie begins.

Remember now, when you went to the counter and picked out all the things you wanted to do, you chose all the very best possibilities. You said to yourself, "Well, the last time I was on Earth, I did this really fabulously wealthy life. I've had a very rich life before, so this time I want to go over there and experience being poor." And they looked at you and said, "Are you sure, wee light?" And you answered, "Oh, yeah, I am so sure. My whole goal is to experience it all. And by the way, in this poor life, I plan to take it to a certain level, and after that, I'll want to do most of it on my own." And you turn around to all in attendance, saying clearly in a loud voice, "I am going to Earth, and I am going to experience what it is to not be very rich, and I don't want anyone interfering with me. I don't want any help, no matter how much I beg, how much I plead, even if I threaten you. Nobody helps me, understand?" The reason for this bold statement is because unless otherwise programmed, we in the world of Guidance will *always* respond. If you but ask at any moment, in any situation, we will respond. Please *never* forget that!

Once you have your programs all set, the new journey begins and you are born into this new body. What happens from here may seem traumatic, yet it is not. Thanks to the ego system, you immediately start the human journey. Everything seems really cold. As hard as you try, you can't speak, and you don't know what to do with these appendages hanging off this thing called a body. You feel like you have just died, when, instead, you have just left the beauty of Light and entered into this human dimension. It takes you a long time to figure this whole process out. Have you ever thought this may be why a baby sleeps so much?

So when you get here, you have it fairly well planned out. You may want to be a doctor or something fancy like that, but you remember on some level that you first need to experience being poor. Well, it may very well be that being poor is not to be a lifelong experience, but only one part of the journey. While on that journey, you repeat the same things over and over to keep you spiraling, so to speak, thereby remaining poor. The only way you will move into the bigger and grander part of that life program is if you see the fullness of the entire journey.

Easy Karma: A Free Meal

Now, I wanted to say all that as a preface for our talk on karma this evening. You see, nowhere in that scenario did you say, "I would like to have one karma of this and two karmas of that and a few of the other." Karma is already registered in your light, my friends. Any karma you may have committed in another lifetime is already programmed into your current blueprint. Each time you take on a new human lifetime, you register the karma that you wish to work on in this lifetime in the cellular consciousness. The karma that you want to deal with from the onset is programmed to be dealt with up front, so to speak. The karma you wish to work with later in your life is also entered into the blueprint at that time. So there it is: your life plan is all set.

Someone says to me, "Kirael, if this life plan is so set, why bother even coming to do it?" That is what you need to understand, my friends. Your life plan is not all that set. Yes, you do know what you want to accomplish. You know what you will focus your energies on. You know the excitement of being here. You just don't remember the thrill of figuring it all out and healing it along the way.

Let me tell you something: If you really want some excitement in this lifetime, you can accumulate a whole bunch of negative karma. For example, you go to a restaurant and you have a waitress who works real hard for you. She brings you a nice meal; she is courteous to you, and everything is going along just grand. Then your bill comes and you look at it. You think, "Oops. She didn't charge me for one of my two dinners." You start justifying the error by saying you will leave her a larger tip than usual. So you enjoy your meal, knowing you will only pay for the meal written on your bill.

Now you ask, "But, Kirael. It's *her* problem. Wasn't it she who made the mistake? Aren't I just getting a break in life?" Be careful not to confuse break with karma. You won't like these two words on the same page. What happened was not a lucky break for you but a mistake that somebody made, and somebody will have to pay for it. If you want to learn more about karma, you can choose to pay for the one meal and go on your way, because you have just created a wee bit of karma.

You say, "All right, Kirael. What would I have to do to get rid of this wee bit of karma that you're talking about?" The only way to eradicate an act of karma is to simply recognize that it is there and begin to work your way out of it. You say, "Wait a minute. How would I do that if I already cheated those people by not paying what I truly owed?" Well, I can think of a number of ways, but I would start by taking a whole bunch of canned foods to the food bank for the people who are in real need of food.

You can do just about anything to clear up karmic acts, by first understanding what you did to create them. Karmic acts are not death sentences. If you wanted to define *karma* in Kirael's dictionary, it would sound like this: *Karma is your right to correct your abilities, to keep a life plan totally aware of the Christ God Light.* Master that and you won't commit negative karma as readily the next time.

You might ask, "Wait a minute, Kirael. Can I really go through life without creating negative karma?" The likelihood is, no, you probably can't, because you are living in a third-dimensional reality that is based in a lot of fear and uncertainty. Most likely, you didn't pay for that other meal because you were afraid you weren't going to have enough money to last you until the next payday. Isn't that possible? You didn't do it intentionally to hurt someone. At least, we would like to hope that. What you did was cover up a fear that you didn't have enough money. And guess what? That fear makes this karma really strong because it is now embedded in the etheric fabric.

Do you know the rule over here? The rule is that *whatever you fear comes upon you.* You might think that it is a bit of a joke or just an old saying, but it is the truth of light, my friends. *What you fear **will** come upon you.*

You say, "God bless you, Kirael. I didn't come over here to feel bad!" Well, you don't have to. Remember what I said about the blueprint in your life program? Everything is changeable, but you have to learn not to throw yourself to the wolves every other day or so. You have to learn not to put yourself in situations where you end up beating the tar out of yourself. When that bill comes to you and it is not complete, take the steps to correct the mistake. Call the waitress over and tell her, "Excuse me, Miss. You made a bit of an error here on the bill." You *know* she will be really happy. Why? Because eventually the cooks would have lined out that meal for her and charged her for it. But if you paid for what you got, then she wouldn't get stuck with that charge.

You say, "I still like the first argument better that it was all the waitress' fault and she deserved it." Well, let me ask each and every one of you if you have ever had the opportunity to make an error in judgment? Have you ever made a wee mistake? I know most of you have. I would venture to say that all of you have. And what if somebody was nice enough to help you undo that mistake in the Now? You say, "Kirael, there you go, backing up. What if that mistake was part of my life plan?" My answer is: There are no plans built on mistakes. There is no such thing as a plan that is made up of mistakes. Every mistake you make is created for a special reason, but no plan is based on mistakes. So if you don't want to enlist this thing called *karma*; if you don't want to put yourself in a position where you will suffer a karmic charge...well, let's look at it from another angle.

I have just used the words "karmic charge." If you knowingly commit an action that creates karma, it creates a charge of energy that is placed in your 90% conscious awareness. It is now in that part of your brain that knows you didn't intend to create karma, yet your 10% allowed it to happen. That karma is now charged in the 90% of your brain whose function is to alleviate itself of any self-created karma. It will most certainly be worked through at the earliest opportunity.

Another kind of karma that you might create is "intentional karma." This takes place when you think through the situation, recognize the potential karmic consequences, and still decide not to pay that wee bill, for example. Now in cases where Lightworkers create intentional karma, there is an even stronger karmic charge to it, with the karmic consequences being about four- to five-fold-deep when they come back to you. You didn't like that one now, right? But hear it again, because most everyone sitting here is what? A Lightworker!

You say, "Wait a minute! Lightworkers are good people, Kirael. You sound like you just punished us." No, I didn't punish you. You and your higher self will work this little deal out. When you create intentional karma, your higher self picks it up and goes, "Darn! This human part of me is just not learning! Well, I'll set up the next lesson three or four layers thick the next time, so that by the time he gets through with that lesson, maybe his 10% awareness won't be so willing to knowingly add up more karma in my energy here." And, God forbid, that you acquire the same karma that you just got nailed for three or four layers thick, because you can really build up some layers on that one. "Layers" meaning whatever it takes for you to get cleared of the karmic situation that you have created. So you see how imperative it is that you understand this.

The Good Book, the one they call the Bible, along with the Koran and most other similar books, tell you in one format or another that there are no free lessons over here. Everything is planned in a certain way, and every plan has a certain outcome that is desirable and not desirable. Which outcome you experience depends on your ability to focus on the truth of what you want. Do not go with intent-filled karma. If you create it, undo it immediately. Your higher self will congratulate you for it. Don't wait until the "karma police" come to get you—and they *will* come and get you, my friends.

Now, one last thing; then we will go to questions. Can you take karma home with you? Yes, you can! You can take karma out of this dimension.

You can take karma home with you through what you call the *death process*—which is really the *alive process*, but what you humans call the death process. If you have a whole bunch of karma accumulated in your system that you haven't cleared, you will take it home with you. After you arrive home, and go through your life review process, guess what? When you return to Earth, you bring the karma along with you so that you can clear it. You say, "Oh, come on, Kirael. Is it possible that we bring those little things called karma back with us?" I would answer it this way: There is no such thing as "little things called karma."

Questions & Answers

Karma Carriers and Healing Karma

When we bring karma back with us in an incarnation, are we magnetically attracted to the people we are karmically indebted to?

KIRAEL: That is a grand question, and probably nobody will like the answer. In fact, I don't know if I am going to have any answers that anybody likes this evening.

The answer is that not only can you attract certain people to you, it is almost guaranteed that you do. So if you don't like somebody in this life, and you create a whole bunch of karma with him or her, that person *will* return with you next time. You will most certainly search out each other's light patterns.

Oh, yes, you will magnetically bring karmic debts with you into each lifetime. You see, you belong to an oversoul, to a family of souls. And in that soul family, of which there could be any number of souls, you all kind of hang out together. So when it is time for you to return to Earth, you go through your entire soul family and ask, "Do I have any karma with you? If so, shall we go back together and work it out?"

Here is something else that you may not want to know about, but I have got to share them all with you tonight. There are people known as *karma carriers*. Let's just say you are my best friend on Earth, and you are a karma carrier. You essentially have come onto the Earth plane to expose people's karma. For example, if you can say little things that aggravate the living you-know-what right out of me, you are a karma carrier, because you know what karma I have got. And because you know that I am not getting rid of my karma very easily, you are going to be of service to me as a karma carrier.

The only reason I bring this up, my friend, is because the next-to-the-last lifetime you were here [addressing the speaker], you did one of those whole karma-carrying things. You came over here and helped all these people with their karma. But you also left a few out, and that is why you are here now.

When we heal this karma, are we given an opportunity to choose how we will do it or does it just depend on how the circumstances present themselves?

KIRAEL: You are always given the opportunity by the higher self to undo the karma, but in the process of undoing it, you have to be careful that you don't create more. The only way to clear karma is through healing. You can't just do a good deed. As I said earlier, if you intentionally didn't pay your full bill at the restaurant, start to heal it by taking some canned goods down to the foodbank, although that only softens the blow. For if you are not going to heal the karma, your higher self will set it up so you can be a little wiser the next time.

The next time, your karma could be set up so that when you buy something and somebody turns their back, you put that something in your pocket instead of paying for it. You may even do this accidentally. Nevertheless, if you decide not to make amends by taking it back, it means that you stole something. So what can you do? Can you take it back and say, "I'm sorry. I need forgiveness. Slap me on the wrist and I'll pay the fine"? Having done that, can you just say, "There, I am off the hook, off the karma, so to speak"? No, you cannot, because you didn't heal it.

The best way to heal karma is to recognize you have committed karma. That is the hardest part for the human world because you like to pretend a lot over here. Once you have realized that you have committed an act of karma, begin the healing process. That means, if there is another human involved, get them involved. You say to the other person, "Look, I did this and I want to heal it. So I need to help *you* help *me* work it out." Then get a mastermind group together; get a group of people to help with your sleepstate programming, prayer and meditation. The main thing is to heal the karma. Then you release it. [For information on Masterminding, Sleepstate Programming, Prayer and Meditation, see Chapter 6]

So what does it feel like to heal karma?

KIRAEL: It feels like you are Light again, except you are still incarnate as a human. This is a good question; I have to give a better answer. How does it feel when you heal a karmic act? It feels like you are standing out in a beautiful meadow, and you see this one tiny little flower that has just poked its head up out of the morning dew. It is sparkling and glistening in the sunlight. You look down at it, and you just know, that is God. That is how it feels.

Karma with Strangers

Is it true that the stronger attraction there is to certain people, the stronger the karma? I mean, do people come into your life because they may be karma carriers? There are people I can meet on the street and I have no energy with them. There are also some that I feel such strong energy with that it almost feels like a confrontation, or that there is something that has to be done with that person. Is that a karmic relationship?

KIRAEL: Oftentimes, yes. This thing about walking down the street, running into someone, and having a karmic exchange or something that releases karma…What do you think the odds are that the person you are interacting with doesn't really exist? The odds are pretty darn high, to be honest with you.

You, in the illusionary world over here, have manifestation powers beyond your wildest dreams. The only problem is that you only like to use them when you don't know you are using them. Those are the times when you use your manifestation powers to the absolute maximum. So if you have a karmic situation, you need what we talked about earlier, a karma carrier. You can create that just through your thought systems alone. You can create that person you accidentally bump into on the street who says, "By the way, I just love the color blue you are wearing," and you get into this conversation, and all of a sudden you feel this release of energy. Or maybe you helped this beautiful little lady with a cane cross the street one day. And maybe you picked up the papers that she dropped and she was all nervous, and you gave her a few kind words. That is repairing karma from other lifetimes. Does that little lady scrambling there with her papers really exist? Chances are only because you created her. You say, "Kirael, that is a little too frightening for me because then you got me to thinking this whole world may not be real." Hello!

So there IS a real reason behind this idea of random acts of kindness!

KIRAEL: Random acts of kindness! Put that on the walls. Put lights on it and do it! When the medium [Rev. Fred Sterling] drives to work every day, he tries to do five random acts of kindness in traffic. But you know what? We caught him saying to one of his angel friends one day, "I'm way behind on my karma. I'm going to do a couple extra today, and see if they don't notice." Come on. Of course, we noticed.

What about karma that you can heal without being aware of the karma involved and karma that you know you can consciously heal? I ask this because you told me in a private session once that I have healed karma that I wasn't even aware of. And I have a feeling it was probably a good thing that I didn't know of it because I probably would have screwed it up if I had. So how can I heal the karma that I know about and not screw it up?

KIRAEL: First of all, let me clarify something. Your statement has to be adjusted a bit. There is no such thing as healing karma you don't know about, for in truth, you know everything. What you are talking about is a level of conscious awareness. When you are totally attuned to the Light of the Creator, it is really easy to know if you are doing something in love or not.

It is easy to know if you are doing something in kindness or in fear. If you are just looking for it such as, "Hmm. Let's see. What can I do to heal karma today? Oh. There is a lady. Let me help her across the street. Oops. She dropped some papers. Let me pick them up for her…" If you spend the entire day that way, you may be missing opportunities to deal with your more serious karmic debts.

You can try instead to see if there is something not working in your life. Let's say that you have a friend who is not one of your most favorite people. Let's say that every time you are around that person you just get an irritated feeling. And when your reaction to that person is usually, "God, what is wrong with her?" I suggest that you not look at the person. Instead, go look in the mirror, because that person is offering you a chance to heal some of your karma.

What karma might that be? Well, you may have spent previous lifetimes being very judgmental, very harsh with people. And now, this person is offering you a chance to act in that same judgmental way again. If you looked at that person and you thought, "Wait a minute. That is a human being just like me. That is a Light of God just like me. She has got a journey just like mine." Then if you looked at her and said, "I love you for your journey. I just don't want to be around you right now," you will have started to heal your karma. That is the only way I can help you, my friend. Heal the karma.

Karma and Gender

Right now, I am doing repair work and renovations for the Easter Seals Foundation. They deal mainly with kids with Down's Syndrome and physical handicaps. Yesterday I met a coordinator speaking to one of these young lads and explaining that the coordinator was going to be leaving. The young boy said that he only trusted women and this particular coordinator. The coordinator said, "But I'm not a woman." And the young boy said, "Yeah, but you have been working here for so long." So my question is, do male energies have more karmic issues than female energies?

KIRAEL: Oh, yeah, you can ask a question like that, I answer it, and then they throw stones at the medium. [*laughter*]

In all seriousness, my friend, there is no rule such as that. You cannot define a male or a female as possibly having more karma than another. The person that you are speaking of obviously has a very strong female orientation. That means that he is very well balanced. That is why you can't define whether a male has more karma than a female.

We know that a male energy acting out a very male orientation likes to throw down a few beers, and whistle at the girls and do things like that. And we know that being judgmental will definitely create a whole bunch of karma. But, believe me, by the same token, there may be some females who are acting out very male-oriented roles as well, and they will create an equal amount of karma. I would say that if you looked at a person who had a very balanced male and female essence, there would still be no way to decide which of the two sides created more karma. It is absolutely impossible.

You also made mention of what they call Down's Syndrome, which is truly more about the child self within an adult body.

Children with Down's Syndrome are so full of love and light that they don't know what is right or wrong.

KIRAEL: Oops. That was a wee little karmic judgment you just created right there. You can heal that one up. I will heal it for you, all right?

These children know more about it than you can imagine, but understand this, my friend: In all sincerity, nine out of every ten children with Down's Syndrome is a divine angel that has incarnated to be of service to you of the human world so that you may discover how to heal your karma.

Karma and "Dark Spirits"

This is a question about good and evil and dark spirits, which doesn't seem to fit with some of the things that you have been saying about karma—about how we come from one life to the next and how we are healing it.

I am thinking about Hitler and what kind of karma he came with. According to some spiritual and positive people in my world that I respect, it is their belief that there are people that come to Earth who are just "dark spirits" and they are just going to stay that way. And their reason is that we need the dark and the light to help us grow. Hitler, for instance, may have actually been a great angel who decided to come here to take it upon himself to get all that hate so that we could learn that we don't want to be like that. The troubling part for me about that is I just want everything to have a happy ending. I don't know why, but I don't want to give up on anybody that I run into in my world that I may think of as a "dark spirit." Yet, the thinking is that is their role to play. So how does karma come into play here?

KIRAEL: Well, actually you answered your own question, for the most part. But I will elaborate on it, if you don't mind. This is a question that comes often to me when I am working with my medium: What about this young fellow named Hitler and others like him? What about all the so-called dark spirits of the world? Let me, first of all, explain something to you: For anything to take any form whatsoever, it must be made of light particles.

If you intensify, or if you "in-densify" (a word I think I made up) light particles and just keep "indensifying" them—bringing them more and more and more tightly compacted together—they will appear to be dark. But believe me, the so-called dark forces that you are talking of are made of the same light that the Light Force is made of. It is with a conscious choice that an energy pattern like Hitler comes here and gives a lifetime that he may clear karma of thousands of other lives by playing out a part that no one else would ever even remotely consider playing. Hitler was playing out a part that would remind people forever that such energy patterns are the most evil of possibilities that exist. But if you can, my friend, remember that no matter what part they are playing, they are made of light.

So you say to me, "I always want everything to come out with a happy ending, but I know it can't, not with everything." Well, that may not be the total truth. Everything can come out with a happy ending, but in this dimension, most of you prefer it not to. Most of you prefer to hold on to certain aspects of the darkened light because you are reminded of the fear.

Now this is going to sound a little confusing, but try it out anyway. Oftentimes, we explore the world of fear so that we never fully engulf ourselves in it. Does that make sense? Oftentimes, we will explore the world through fear so as not to have to "indensify" ourselves to the point where we have to act out the fear or to be the fear. The "Hitlers" of the world became the fear. Hitler became the fear in order that everyone today would remember that name and that vision of that light particle group to be reinstated, and to know that they never want to enter into that darkened light again. And for that, he paid the price. For the price he paid, believe me, the karma that was washed off of considerable lives was immeasurable.

Let's move on to someone in your reality. For example, let's look at a person that does you a disservice or harms you in some way. You can, if you like, try to fix that person, but you know my patent statement on this: If you would focus solely on lighting up your own life so brightly, that person you want to fix would be fixed by being in your light. That is all it would take. Then you would have a happy ending.

When you are totally thrilled with your light, the people around you begin to be totally thrilled with their light. When you are totally abundant, the people around you become totally abundant; that is, you create a collective consciousness, and then the density of fear cannot vibrate. Do you understand? It takes a vibration of fear for fear to exist. Through a culmination of light particles, you can emit positive light by your thinking processes alone that can dissipate the density of fear. So it can come out with a great ending every time. I think, my friend, you are fairly good living proof of that.

I think I understand my role better now in my interactions with others. But what about the interaction between these so-called evil forces and other people, the victims of Hitler for example? Or maybe a person gets raped by someone and another person is witness to it. We are told not to hate a person who has done very hurtful things to another.

KIRAEL: Hate the act, but don't hate the person. That is the only way out of it, my friend, because some deeds are so vile that your human consciousness cannot get past them. Yes, hate the deed and let the person be lit up.

Karma in Creation

There is a story in Hinduism about a saint who has something like skin cancer on his arm. He goes to his physician who cuts out the cancer without administering any kind of anesthesia. The story goes that this saint says during the procedure, "Oh, poor arm, you have this illness. We are going to fix it," as though the body has its own karma. So I am wondering if only people have karma? Do bodies have karma? Do rocks have karma? Or is karma just a human condition?

KIRAEL: Every creation of the Creator is capable of karma. By the time you choose to be an enlightened being or a lighted essence of the Earth, you will choose to no longer create karma. In essence, karma will usually exist only in your highly evolving societies.

For instance, grass is God's creature, yes? Do you think that the lawn mower creates karma when it cuts down the grass? No, it doesn't. But let me tell you what does happen. Because of the interaction of all light, the minute that lawn mower starts onto that plot of grass, every blade that it comes into contact with immediately sends out a signal to every other blade of grass. The signal is one of celebration. You say, "Wait a minute. The grass is about to be cut in half. I don't know what you'd be celebrating." But you have to understand that when it sends out that signal amongst all of the grass, that grass is being told, "We are about to get a new life. We are about to be cut in half so that we can grow quicker and stronger," so the roots get more excited. It doesn't matter whether the grass is five inches tall or spread across five hundred acres. Collectively, the grass knows that the mower is out and it is excited, for it is being given an opportunity for growth and new life again.

Here is the answer to your question on whether only humans experience karma: The only ones to use the karmic system are energies that are evolving, those that are trying to return to or go beyond a certain level of awareness. The grass, for instance, only stays grass as long as it wants to stay grass; it does not have a desire to be a dandelion. You see, without the desire to evolve into a new awareness, there is no karma. Do you see that beautiful tree out there? That tree picks up no karma. However, if a pet dog bites you, karma! And it will remain a dog for a long time. So here is the answer to your question: Only in evolutionary processes does karma exist.

Does that mean that grass is not ever going to evolve into being a dog?

KIRAEL: Pretty much so. The grass is grass, yes. And it is not always greener on the other side!

So does the body have its own karma that exists independently of mine?

KIRAEL: Now, that is an interesting question, for when you realize the body is a vibratory structure of your thought processing, it will not be independent. Your thinking allows that body to stand in front of the microphone. Your thinking decides how wide it is going to be, how tall it is going to be. Your thinking decides every aspect of that body. So if the karma issue in your light wants to experience skin cancer as opposed to going through a great big cancer in your stomach, it puts a little wee skin cancer out there on your finger so you can see it. Then you can heal it. But the point is that the arm does not become unconscious of the rest of the body, unless you are capable of willing it so. Then it can be considered to be karmically on its own.

Karma and Ego

What is the relationship between karma and ego?

KIRAEL: That is a good question. And the answer is simply...nothing.

Nothing?

KIRAEL: No, but I will define it. When you come to the clarity that the ego is a self-induced layer of energy, or layer of light particle energy, that allows you to pretend that you are not what you are but who you think you are, then you become aware that this induced energy has nothing to do with your karma. It has nothing to do with your karma other than allowing you to be held here in a state of light "particle-ization" whereby you, through the process called "body human," can then act out the karmic situations. In essence, the ego and the karma have no relationship whatsoever to each other.

You say, "Well, don't egotistical people make more karma than others?" No, absolutely not. Egotistical persons are not always as bad off as you might think they are. You are not going to like what I am about to say, but as a rule, egotistical persons are those who are coming to a clarity in their lives that they are in control. In that light, egotistical people utilize the clarity of who they are to an advantage. They move beyond the ego's controlling system and allow the karmic issues to be healed in their light. Does that make sense? That is how the ego and karma are connected.

So it is best then to just heal the karma?

KIRAEL: Don't heal your ego; there is nothing to heal. But do heal the karma.

Karma, Lawyers and Politicians

Are lawyers and politicians karma carriers?

KIRAEL: Ha! Lawyers and politicians? This is going to get me in as much trouble as I want to get into this evening. I would say that as a rule, a fair portion of your lawyers and politicians are relatively younger souls. Isn't it a fact that your politicians are normally lawyers and your lawyers are normally politicians? Because of that, they have a tendency to build up and work with a lot of karma. Therefore, you could consider them as karma carriers, yet they are not designed for that role. They pick up karma along the way.

So regarding the results of the United States Presidential election in the year 2000, is this a chance for the masses to heal certain karma?

KIRAEL: I think that is a given, right? That is a given *yes* to your given question. But will it happen, my friend? Last year in December, I told you what would happen in the Presidential election, and everybody said, "Nah, nah, don't worry about it." And I don't want you to worry about it. But I do want you to be clear that the guides and the angels are setting up your beautiful world so that you in the human light can recognize how you have been falsely shown different possibilities.

When I told you last year that the election would be one of the most fantastic ones you had ever seen, everybody said, "Oh, tell us what is going to happen, Kirael. Is the Green Party going to get elected?" And I did not tell you, did I? Because would I not have taken all the fun away for you? You wouldn't have been able to sit up till midnight wondering, "Who is the next president?" Well, the first thing you have to realize is that they [Gore and Bush] are both working for the same energy anyway, so it doesn't really matter.

You, the people, have to stand up and take a good hard look at what is happening. Don't be too concerned about the outcome as that will be karmically driven throughout all the processes involved. Instead, you, the people, need to stand and look, and say, "What are my questions now? And will I get an answer?" And don't stop until you do. When you get the answers you are satisfied with, then you karmically release and heal yourself. This is because every one of you in America got tainted by this election; you just don't know how deeply yet.

Karma in Other Dimensions

Is karma an energy that occurs in just duality consciousness dimensions or is it a cosmic law throughout the universes and dimensions, throughout all creation?

KIRAEL: Karma is a cosmic law that exists throughout all universes, if you will, but you have varying degrees of it. All of you here in the Earth plane are able to experience the densest degree of karma because you get to act out the process. That is one of the fun things about coming to Earth. I know you don't agree with me, but it is. It is fun to come here and create some karma, and then clean it up. It feels really good.

Here is a fine example: We have in other reality forces the Sirians and the Pleiadians, with the Sirians being a wee bit younger in their force light than the Pleiadians. If they looked back on all that they had experienced in all of their lifetimes and decided they really wanted to experience karma, they would seek out a host here on the Earth plane. That is, they would borrow a human being to experience karma because it is only at this level on Earth that you have the purest karmic experience. Anything else would be watered down, so to speak.

Karma is a universal process that is available on all levels. At higher levels of consciousness, karma takes on other forms of experience. For instance, the angelic realm does not honor karmic issues any longer. If an angel is operating in the angelic world and sees the potential of a karmic act that could be experienced more thoroughly, it will simply incarnate into the Earth plane and do it here. Angels can still see karma; they just can't deal with it in their dimension. How do you like that?

No Intent, No Karma

Let's say I know I have karmic issues with another person that need to be healed. And let's say the other person, my brother, isn't aware of the karma on the same conscious level. Is that because he has already healed the karma relating to that situation? How do you heal in a situation like that?

KIRAEL: It could be either way, my friend. It could be that your brother has so "indensified" the situation that he can't recognize the karma because he is not willing to deal with it. It could also be as you said, that he has cleared his karmic portion of it and, therefore, can just stand in that light and not be faltered by it.

Another possibility also exists that it doesn't make any difference whether he is aware of the karma between you, because you, who recognized the karma, are the only one that needs to deal with it at that time. Going back to my opening statement with the waitress and the check, if you paid your bill but didn't realize that she hadn't added up the check properly, you would not have committed any karma. At this point, the only one who may have committed some karma is the one who wrote out the check. As a karma carrier, she may have been trying to define her own world by creating a space where karma could exist. But you, the one who paid the bill and didn't realize the error was there, are karma-free.

You might say, "Well, all right then, I just won't ever add up my bills anymore." This is not a bad idea in a sense, because if you unwittingly commit karma, karma doesn't exist. In other words, in order to commit karma, it has to be done knowingly. But once you do so, the only way to heal it is by recognizing the karmic issues that you are evolving through. It makes no difference who the players are. The only thing that matters is your ability to evolve through this soul level by recognizing and healing the karma that is there.

Karma and Diet

When you were talking about grass, I thought about animals. I know this is a controversial issue, but do we create karma when we kill and eat animals?

KIRAEL: I will tell you this: There are animals that are non-evolutionary, and if you think your question is controversial, listen to the answer. For all of you who like eating hamburgers, I said in my first book [*Kirael: The Great Shift*] that you would be a little unhappy to know that cows are no longer evolutionary animals. They have evolved to the highest state that they can. If, however, you go out and eat your kitty cat, now you are really setting yourself up for some karma because cats are an evolving species of animals. In other words, eating beef is possibly on the same level as eating a bale of hay, so to speak, because cows are not an evolving society of energy. So, there are certain animals that you will incur less karma with. That is the "legal" answer.

But now let me give you the answer that I really want to share with you—the good answer. For the most part, the karma that you are committing when you eat meat will be evidenced by the demands it places on the physical body. The karma is what you are doing to your body, and that is karma that only *you* can heal. So eat the animals; chance the karma.

I have heard that our intestines were designed to digest vegetables and grains, and that it is a disease-producing situation to eat meats. Is that true?

KIRAEL: Remember when I leave, you will need to deal with the medium. I know the medium will want to run right out and grab a hamburger after this because it is going to be playing in his mind. But don't let him, all right? [*laughter*]

In all seriousness, you need to be very clear that the body process was made in God's Light of Light as part of the whole, lighted process. When you read my book [*Kirael Volume II: The Genesis Matrix*], you will get a clearer understanding of how Adam and Eve, "Atom and Eve-olution," came to be. The Creator didn't put the animals there for Adam and Eve to eat; It put them there to do other things, but things got carried away over a long period of time.

In truth, the Creator made the physical body to exist on non-evolutionary food sources. That would be more of your plant products, of course. The physical body never does well with the intake of a lot of red meats. Because if you eat red meat, you are eating something that very likely has something wrong with it. Don't measure a soybean to a piece of cow flesh. You will not like the measure.

So am I okay if I eat chicken and fish?

KIRAEL: Well, the chicken and fish are not real happy about it. It is all in your own understanding of light. Hear this clearly, and it is not a cop-out answer. The Creator put all the levels together and left it for you to decide what is best for you. And if you feel that you can ingest a big, fat cow and feel good afterwards, then your body will just have to work harder.

In short, my answer remains the same: It is still the free choice of the human. Your belief systems truly control the outcome of such acts.

"Dark Angels"

When angels on the side of good try to help out humankind, do they create karma? How do angels become "fallen angels"?

KIRAEL: I will answer it this way: If angels processing as "incarnate angels" in the evolutionary system were construed as "fallen angels," then I would grant you that they are susceptible to karma. They probably came here in order to work on that. On the other hand, the "light angels" in your midst this evening are here, not so much to guide, but to answer your questions to the best of their ability. And always do those of the angel world stay in truth.

As for those so-called "dark angels," you will probably not like the answer. Your so-called "dark angels" are a figment of your imagination. You create them so that you can have an excuse to do the dirty deed that you want to do and then say, "The angels made me do it." But know this: they are created in your mind; therefore, as long as you think they exist, they do.

ET's and Karma

What about the ET's, the extra-terrestrials, that have been involved in cattle mutilations and so on?

KIRAEL: Well, first, you must realize that what was happening then is not happening now. You are referring to some past events that involved a group of extra-terrestrials known as the *Greys*. In simple terms, they were very low vibrators that had stolen the secrets and the understandings from the high vibrators. And, yes, it is true that they entered into your Earth plane and actually did those things that you referred to.

Let me also tell you about the planet Zenith. Zenith is somewhat of a replica of the Earth process in that there is a gravitational force on Zenith. They don't do the third-dimensional things, but are more fourth- and some fifth-dimensional energy patterns of lights. But even amongst the lower vibrators of that awareness, there are still karmic issues being played out. At the same time, the more highly evolved species on Zenith have vibrated beyond that. They no longer involve themselves in anything that would create karma because they have already learned the lessons that karma creates. But believe me, my friend, there are planetary systems out there that are not as evolved as yours. Truth is that you are only about eighteen million light years away from a planetary system where dinosaurs exist even today.

Clearing Karma: Baptism

Did Master Jesus have karma at the time just prior to his crucifixion?

KIRAEL: By that time, Master Jesus did not exist. Master Jesus was the Christ Light, and karma does not ensue from Light. You cannot create karma within the Light. Remember that the death experience for Master Jesus was when he walked into the River Jordan and became the Host of the Christ Light. From that point on, no karma could ensue. This is why he would almost always speak in parables after he walked into the river and was baptized, for parables allow the listeners to identify with what you have said through their own thought processes. That was the day he cleared all karmic issues. From that day forward, anything that would have appeared to be karmically inclined would be a figment of the imagination of the one looking for anything possibly karmic in nature.

Then is baptism a way of clearing karma?

KIRAEL: Baptism is the clearing of karma. Oh! Now everybody will be lined up down the hall telling the medium, "Please baptize me right here!" [*laughter*]

In truth, if you would decide to stand before your minister to receive the Light of Christ in you in baptism, and if you would fully enlighten yourself to that Light, you would clear all karma. But as a rule, you, being evolutionary in the human world, will not clear to that level. You will only clear to the level that you feel comfortable clearing to.

When the medium puts a minister on each side of you, creating a trinity force which is the creation of the Creator's Love, and when he places some water upon you and prays for a speck or light particle of the Christ Light to reignite the Christ Light within you, thereby creating that infusion of love, you could literally eradicate all karma at that point. But will you? Likely not. Still, you would be better off than you were. I promise you that.

Karma in War Time

Let's say you are a soldier sent into war and your job is to kill people and win the war. When you are in a position where you believe that what you are doing is right and you feel that you are right, how does that affect the karma that you create for yourself as opposed to someone who thinks that what they are doing is wrong?

KIRAEL: The answer would be very clear, my friend, for you use the words "you feel that you are right." In order not to incur karma, you would have to *know* that you are right. If we took all these soldiers fighting amongst each other and we got them to know that it is okay to kill each other; that it is okay to kill the Creator, and that it is okay to kill God; then each time they looked down the barrel and fired at one of their brothers or sisters, they would have to know that they were killing a wee piece of the Creator. Now that is too far-fetched for the human mind to deal with in the middle of a grand war, right?

And everybody thinks that they are fighting for the right cause. God gets invoked on all sides of all wars.

KIRAEL: And then everybody fights to save the Creator's name. Policemen, army folks and others along this line. Isn't that amazing to think that if you *know* what you are doing is in the name of the Creator's Light and in love, no karma is attached? Well, if you have been given a whole bunch of rhetoric and you truly believe in what you are doing, the karma is minimal, but it is there. If you were fully enlightened, if you were fully aware of your lightness, you couldn't pull the trigger. You simply couldn't. I mean, it would be virtually impossible for a being of light to pull the trigger. Because the love is there.

So, it is a fine line you got me dancing on here. But it is true: it is a dance. Many people, including my medium, went to war. You [addressing the speaker] went to war. You know it is not the most beautiful thing. Yet, it happened; it was done. But the karma that you picked up there, my friend, is eradicated upon remembering that what you did was a snow job that you were led to believe. And once you release it from that level, once you become aware that you can heal it inside of you, then the healing is but a beginning. And that is when all the acts of karma can be eradicated. Does this make sense? God bless you, my friend. And I know that your acts of karma are passing quickly.

Closing Statement

Here is what I want to make very clear: Karma is almost always committed against one of your brothers or sisters. Now if you go to the reality of that statement, is it not the truth that every time you commit an act of karma you commit it unto yourself? Because you *are* your brothers and sisters.

Have you heard that little story about the light particle who volunteered to incarnate with another, essentially to help him clear his karma? Look about you. Others in this gathering just might be here to help you through all of your karma. Or you just might be married to your karma carrier. For those of you thinking, "Oh, I finally got one for my husband now," be careful. You might want to think twice before telling him, "You know how fortunate you are? I am your karma!" Because you just created karma, my friend!

Well, it is time that I be on me way. I want to thank all of you for coming out. I have enjoyed ever so much being here this evening. Next time we come together, let's have another exciting subject to share.

Good evening to all of you.

5 *THE TRUTH ABOUT YOUR RELATIONSHIPS*

Opening Statement

KIRAEL: Good evening.

This evening's event is based around the reality of relationships. To begin with, all should become aware that this thing we call relationships is much deeper than most people realize. Relationships, my friends, are a wee bit more than just about the husband and the wife, the boyfriend and the girlfriend, the employer and the employee, the Creator and all of the Creator's beautiful children. They are about relationships throughout all worlds.

We are here to learn the truth about relationships—to unmask these relationships, if you will. When we unmask this energy of relationships, the question arises: Who must be unmasked? It is the self, my friends. So this night, as we gather our energies in alliance on this particular subject, let each of us become aware of what we are really looking for. This would be the relationship within ourselves, for if we are to conquer any relationship in the world, it is first about the self.

Let's speak for a moment about the Guidance Realm from which I hail. Most of you are aware that I come from a place that we refer to as the Seventh Reality, or Seventh Dimension. There are those who ask of me, "Kirael, could you tell me what the Seventh Dimension looks like?" Well, if I am to answer that, I would first ask each of you a similar question, "What does the Third Dimension look like?" How would you explain that? You see? You can't. Yes, you can tell me what *happens* in the Third Dimension. You can describe the illusion that you experience in the Third Dimension, but you can't tell me what the Third Dimension *looks* like. And I will tell you why: the Third Dimension is an illusion as are all the other dimensions.

The Third Dimension is a holographic-type state of energy patterns so comprised in the energy of thought that they only become understandable within the linear space of laying one reality on top of another. So if you take this *real* world of the Third Dimension and you bring it into one space, it is simply comprised of illusions. I mean that every single thing that happens in your world is simply the understanding of a thought vibration that has been amplified with enough deep passion to allow it to become a so-called *reality*.

Base Your Relationships on Truth

Relationships differ not. Let's look at a relationship between two entities, for example, between a male and a female (not that we want to limit it to that). Most relationships on the Earth plane have come together in one fashion or another in the world of untruth. What I mean to say is that oftentimes, when one enters the field of dating with the idea of carrying on a steady romance that may lead to marriage, the initial contact is based on appearances, which hold many untruths.

Now you say, "Well, how serious are these untruths, Kirael?" I will give you this as an example: Look at all the beautiful women sitting around the room here this evening. How many of you are aware of this thing they call makeup? Well, right there you find the first wee bit of untruth. How many of you have dressed this evening to impress someone else? There is another wee bit of untruth. You say, "Kirael, you are being a bit stringent with us." I say, "Yes, I am." For I want to establish truth beyond anything that you have ever experienced.

One of the most infamous untruths over here is the way that many people will ask a question or make a statement so that it will elicit a desired result. They are not necessarily looking for the truth. What they are looking for is a desired response. So you ask your questions or you make your statements based along this line. Yet if you were to really look inside yourself and ask what it is that you want to know, or what it is that you are asking, the truth becomes evident. So you say, "But Kirael, what if I am the only one in the whole of the world that is telling the truth and everyone else is asking questions?" Then I say, "Congratulations, you are where we must start." Just like the Master Jesus. In the whole of the world, Master Jesus, who was one of the most predominant healers, was always in truth, my friends.

What about your relationship with your employers or your employees? How many people might be guilty of a little white lie here and there? How many of you call up your boss on some mornings saying, "*Cough, cough.* I don't feel so good," when in fact you are feeling great, but you just want to take the day off? "Well," you say, "that is done all over the place, Kirael. It is accepted." Accepted by whom? You see, that is the question.

So then we go to the employer, and we say, "Mr. Employer, why is it that your people have to call you and fib to you? Why don't you understand them dearly enough that they might be able to call you up and say, 'You know what, Mr. Employer? I just don't feel like coming to work today. Is it all right?'" And the employer says, "Yes, that's fine. Go ahead and take the day off."

You are thinking that I am reaching there, aren't you? Well, I am actually talking about truth. What if a company actually operated that way? Do you know the first thing that would happen? You would not be calling up and saying, "*Cough, cough.* I don't feel good today." You wouldn't do it. You would simply go to work the way you are supposed to.

This is my point: What if you were to have a relationship where nobody, but nobody, could tell a fib? What if you and your children had a relationship based on the totality of truth? You say, "Oh, I have got that, Kirael. My son and my daughter never fib to me." Don't take a vote, my friends. Don't take up a vote there because you might find you are not in a winning space.

So what am I trying to say? I am saying that your world is perfect as it is. And if you want to make it more palatable, all you have to do is make a few changes. Well, you say, "It's not easy, Kirael. If I start telling the truth and everybody else is fibbing, I am going to be a wee bit out of place." Well, yes, in fact, you might be, but I tell you this: You are going to sleep a lot better. You are going to think a lot clearer. You are just plain going to feel good.

So you say, "Okay, Kirael. What then is the challenge?" The challenge is to tell the truth. If you are to unmask your relationships, don't try to unmask the other person. Unmask your own reality. Take your own mask off. You say, "Well, Kirael, what if I take my mask off and they don't like who I am?" Well, maybe the relationship should come to an end. Wouldn't you think so? Can you imagine, my friends, a relationship where one was in total, total honesty; where you didn't have to pull any punches? Wouldn't that be a beautiful thing?

Let's take this perfect relationship that I am speaking of and ask, Who must start the process? Well, you know the answer is that each individual must start. You will need to sit down with your mate, and say, "Okay, here is what we want to do. We are going to draw a line in the proverbial sand of life, and we are not going back over that line again. We are both going to step over the line together and from there, in every moment, we shall always tell the truth. We shall never exaggerate the truth one iota."

You say, "But, Kirael, what about all of the history we share? What about our pasts that created this relationship?" Well, if you are living your relationship on history, then there might be something wrong with that relationship. What if you started brand-new? You say, "But, Kirael, my wife and I have been married for 10 years, and now you want us to talk like there is no history?" Yes, pretty much so because I am going to tell you something, my friends: In the not-so-distant future you won't be looking back at much of your history at all. You will be looking at what is in your life at the moment. Where is the thrill of your life this very second? You say, "Well, we will just live a fantasy." No, you are to live a reality—a reality based on the illusion that you create in the Now.

Think about it. What if each and every one of you could draw that line with your mate? Or even with just a friend? What if you could step across the line and have no history? The only way you could stay on that side of the line would be to never tell an untruth again, because the minute you told an untruth, you would have to go back across the line. How many people would stay on the new side?

You say, "Well, Kirael, might you give us a week or so to practice?" I also might say, "Yes," but I don't know if you really should take that much time. I think you should make a commitment, a commitment to the God Light Truth. Ooh, there's a fancy one! "What is the God Light Truth?" you ask. The God Light Truth is when you check with your heart before you open your wee mouth, and whatever comes from your heart is what you say unto the world. That is the God Light Truth.

This is one of me favorites: When someone says to you, "How do you like my new hairdo?" You say, "You see, Kirael? Right there, I have got to fib because I don't want to make her feel too badly." Well, can't you say something without making her feel so badly? Can't you say, "If you like your new hairdo, by golly, I like it just as well"? You say, "But what if I don't like it, Kirael?" Well, why wouldn't you? Why wouldn't you like someone else's hairdo? You would have to go into judgment at that point, wouldn't you? And you very well know the Creator doesn't want you to do that!

What if, my friends, this awesome experience called the Creator is not some judging entity that everybody has made It out to be? What if this beautiful world of the Creator is pure, pure, pure, love? The Creator has no energy for judgment whatsoever. It looks at every single thing that you do and thinks, "What a grand lesson!"

What if our Creator isn't sitting up there in the proverbial cloudworks of the skies, surrounded by a bunch of angels playing harps, while trying to figure out what you are doing that is right and wrong? What if this beautiful world of the Creator just glows upon you at every opportunity and allows for you to see the beauty of your own reality? What if you began looking at your fellow human beings the same way? What if everybody in this room and throughout the world that is listening to me words just simply took a stand and said, "From here on out, I am not going to judge another soul as long as I live"? What if, my friends?

You might say, "What about that little fellow in the chat room over here that is using foul language? Should we not judge him?" I think you might have great sympathy for him. At the same time, understand that if you have to use fouled-up language to make a point, you might want to look at that. Maybe you need to find more impassioned words than curses. You say, "Well, Kirael, it has been that way for a long time." My friends, that would be an excuse. And if you live on excuses, that creates a whole new journey.

So what am I saying to you? I am saying, let's return the world to love, starting right here with everyone in this room as well as with everybody listening over the Internet. Why don't we start a new world today, a world of love and truth? What if we decided never to lie again? What would everybody in this room be stuck doing right now? As I look around, I see a few of you in relationships here—holding hands and things like that. What if you had to turn to your friend right now and say, "I am drawing the line. I am drawing the line in the sand. Would you like to cross over with me?" That would mean you would get to start over, brand-new, fresh and clear.

Don't step over the line until you are ready. But when you do step over the line, I promise you something: You will have a relationship that lasts for life. And never would that relationship be put asunder; you will carry it through for as long as you live. You say, "Well, I don't know, Kirael. I think you are asking a wee bit much of us." And I say, "Yes, you know I am."

So how do we unmask the beauty of relationships? You do it from the truth of love. Stop asking your friends and your relatives to be something that they are not. Don't ask them to be what you want them to be. Accept them for what they are or get away from the relationship. Did you hear that? *Accept them for what they are.* You say, "But, Kirael, what if I want to help them grow?" My friend, you don't have that right. You can offer them light and you can set an example. If they want to follow, congratulations to them and to you, but you can't make them change by demanding it.

It is the same with the way you bring up your children, my friends. You can't demand that they be good. You can only hope that you set a good enough example. When you see them doing something wrong, look deep inside yourself and ask yourself, "Where did they learn that little trick they just did?" And lo and behold, most often, you will find it down there inside of you somewhere.

Am I making it sound pretty downcast this evening? I am talking to many new friends for the first time who are thinking, "Boy, this Kirael is a really rough energy, isn't he?" No, I am not. I just know what the world needs. I know what your angelic brothers and sisters want. I know what your galactic brothers and sisters want. I know what they all want. They all want us to come to truth because when you are in Truth, the Trust and Passion follow right behind.

Try it out, my friends. Here is a challenge for you: Try it for seven days. For seven days I would like you to go without judgment and without telling even so much as a wee white lie. No judgment and no fibbing! Seven days! At the end of that time, if you don't like it, you can come back and look me up. Don't talk to my medium; talk to me. Some of you are already reaching for the masking tape to cover up your mouth. I know you are, for some of you are figuring that is the only way you can do it.

What if, my friends, you didn't succeed, but you tried? Do you realize that the Earth plane would immediately be a better place? You say, "Just by little ol' me doing that?" Yes, just by little old you doing that. The truth is this: once you have gone there and stepped over the line into the world of truth, the whole world eventually goes with you because, remember, the world is your illusion. When you make your changes, the world changes with you. That's pretty fancy, huh?

We are going to open this evening up to questions. We can talk about anything this evening. It is just family here and family around the world.

Questions & Answers

What is There to Fear?

What you have shared is very difficult to do—to be in truth with the self. As for me, it is difficult because of the fears that I hold on to. So can you help me? Can you help us to move past those fears which are within our cellular consciousness?

When you think back 2000 years ago, Master Jesus was in total truth, and look what happened to him. The witches in Salem were in total truth, and they got killed for it. So, there appears to be a correlation between speaking the truth and being killed for it. I also know that things are changing with the light energy that is moving into the Earth plane, yet, because of our cellular memory, we are healing our fears. Do you have any insights into this?

KIRAEL: I will be happy to address that. If you have to understand one thing about fear, understand that you didn't have any when you got here. Instead, you have had to learn it along the way, and your teachers have done a pretty good job of teaching you. Who are your teachers? Your teachers started out with your mommy and daddy, and then those in your schooling, and in your religious world, and then others in the business world. But everybody has taught you from fear. They taught you the fear of what would happen if you didn't do something a certain way.

Many of you are in a relationship because you are afraid of what is outside of the relationship. You are afraid of being alone because you can't find a relationship within yourself. Instead, you depend on someone else to fill in your relationship reality. You know what I mean by that, right? If you don't have a good relationship with yourself—that is, if your rapport with yourself is missing this great love within yourself—you fill that with the love of someone else. But when they don't give it exactly the way you want it, you start pretending that you will get it a different way. Next, you start doing all sorts of different maneuvers in order to maintain the love that you think you are getting from someone else, when in truth, you are probably not getting any love from them anyway. If you have to try to get love from your mate, then that mate likely doesn't have a lot of love inside either, so you are trying to get the proverbial blood from a stone, aren't you?

What is the fear that you exist in? I will give you a couple of examples. Let's suppose that this young man wants to say hello to that young lady. What is his basic fear? His basic fear is that she is going to shun him. He fears that she is going to say something like, "Oh, you are too big and stupid to talk to me." How many times do you build up the fears in your thinking process? How many people won't call up somebody because they are afraid of what is going to be said?

So I want to address your question this way: In the first place, you have to learn fears; and if you have learned them, you can unlearn them. The only way to unlearn them, my friend, is to trust in your Creator Light. It is to trust that if you do everything you are supposed to do, then whatever fears you have will be overcome by the Light. And if you don't have that trust, then you need to keep working towards it.

So the truth is the truth. You have heard this before. Take every fear you have, face it, and embrace it. And what you will find is what you feared really doesn't exist. Once you figure that out, all fears begin to evaporate.

What is the one thing they tell you over here on your Earth plane? "The man to fear the most is the man who has nothing that you can take away." That's the man to fear the most. When you can't threaten a man by putting him in jail, and when you can't threaten a man by taking away whatever he has, because he has nothing, then you will find a man with no fear.

Truth at Work

Tonight's topic on truth is something I work with a lot. In fact, I have in this past week dealt with several personnel issues at work that required a lot of truth on my part.

KIRAEL: Good.

My business is sales, and truth is something that I think I am the best at, so I would like some feedback on how I am doing.

KIRAEL: Well, I will give you this feedback. First of all, we will let everybody know that you have a destiny with the United States government, meaning that you are an employee of the government. Along with that, you are also what I would consider, my friend, one of the first in the car sales business that has the Light of Truth as your guidance factor. So I can only say this, my friend: You are in for a hard road.

Now, that wasn't good, was it, Kirael? No, but I will explain. You are in for a hard road because you are trying to take on two worlds that exist on so many untruths that they have built their entire realities for the most part on these untruths, and you are looking to be the Light inside of them. That is a hard road, my friend. If anything, I would like to get you a halo—if they had them over here. Still, if you had them, I would have you wear one so people would ask you, "What is that thing surrounding your head like that?" And you would say, "Kirael gave that to me because I am trying to tell the truth."

You say, "Wait a minute, Kirael. How come you say I am *trying* to tell the truth?" Because you have got how many years experience at doing it the other way, so you are bound to slip up every now and then. Not with intent on your part; it just happens. So you say, "Well, then, how good am I?" You are good because you are trying. If people would stop worrying about succeeding and just try to succeed, they would already be successful. Does that make sense?

Yes.

KIRAEL: Simply work at succeeding, and you are a success. The simple truth is that nobody comes here to this Earth plane to succeed. This is a hard one for you in the human world to understand. Nobody comes over here to be perfect. Everybody comes here to the Earth plane to experience success along the path. Everybody comes here to move towards perfection, and there is such a giant difference in the two. I am not playing a word game with you. It is the truth.

I say to you simply: If you want, I will give you a score card that you can keep along the way. You can look at it every night before you go to bed. You can sit down and count up all of the blessed things that happened to you that day—the little things, such as you saw a tree, you smelled a flower, you sold a car—all of the little things. Then at the end of that day, you look right up into the Light of the God Creator and you say, "We did it together."

When you get there, my friend, you and all the other people will stop telling God, "God, you have to do this for me and you have to do that for me." You will instead get to the light of saying, "Me and the Creator had a good one today." And you know what? If you had a bad day, you can say, "Me and the Creator, we had a bad one today. But I bet if I just pray a little bit and ask for a wee bit more light on the whole process, I will get it in the morrow." Then, you will be working toward the perfection.

Stepping Over the Line

What about the karmic issues of a relationship and what we come here to learn? You told me once that the heaviest karmic issues were between a parent and a child. Now if I do what you suggest, and cross over that line and put everything behind me, would those karmic issues be healed? Would they be fulfilled or learned, or whatever the term might be?

KIRAEL: Believe it or not, my friend, if both you and your child stepped over the line together in love and in truth, the karmic issues would—I stress *would*—be eradicated. This is because you would understand that those karmic issues don't exist, except in the grudges that you hold and in the untruths that have not been fulfilled. From that day, you would begin the new journey of a lifelong love that would literally heal all of the karma.

So does it have to be a joint commitment?

KIRAEL: Let me rephrase it a bit. I would say that if you and the daughter or the son, stepped across the line together, and you became in truth and in love, but the other one didn't, then *your* karmic issues would be erased, while the other's would have just doubled.

If you walk across the line of truth and the first thing you do is become untruthful, you are creating a situation of fear—exactly what the first question was about tonight. How do we do that? Well, the first thing you usually do is become afraid. So your first thought is, "Do you think they will know I told an untruth?" Then you know what you have to do next, don't you? You have to tell another untruth to cover up the first one, and it never stops. So you end up in the downslide.

Okay. Another question. I did as you suggested and I imagined myself stepping over the line, but I found that there was nothing to hold on to. That in itself is scary, so what do I do at that point?

KIRAEL: Well, here comes an answer a lot of people won't like: You *do* have something to hold onto—the Creator Light and the love of yourself. With those two, my friend, you don't need anything else to hang on to. When you come to the total belief and the total love of your Creator's essence—because that is *your* essence—and when you come in love, there is nothing you need to hold onto. Nothing! Because at any given moment, you can rise right up into the Creator's Light and let all of this Third Dimension go behind you.

Can you imagine no fear of death? A lot of people over here tell me, "Kirael, I don't have any fear of death." That is, except when death approaches them and they say, "Wait, wait, wait. Let me get ahold of Master Kirael. Let's talk about it." But what happened to the "I don't have any fear of death stuff"?

My friend, I want to make this clear, because that is such a grand question. If you step over the line and you see nothing to hold onto, then you really haven't stepped all the way over the line. You see, Truth creates Trust, and Trust together with Truth is your Passion.

Once you step over that line, you cannot fall if you step all of the way. But what most people do is stick a wee toe over the edge of the line. They say, "There, I'm in. Let me look next to me and see my partner. Let me see how far over his toe is." Then you say, "Let's see, my toe is a wee bit further over the line than his is, so I'm going to wait for him. In fact, I'm not only going to wait for him; I'm going to give him a hard time about getting up here with me."

Instead, why not tell your partner, "We're making an agreement here, and no matter what, I'm keeping the agreement. No matter what. I'm not even going to have my eyes open to see if you step with me. I'm going to close my eyes in pure faith, pure truth, and pure trust. I'm stepping over that line, and if you're there when I get over there, hallelujah. If you're not, see ya." Then step across.

Before I do that, do I need to have a certain level of self-love?

KIRAEL: Yes. And guess where you are going to get it? Inside yourself. Stop looking outside for it and look inside. There is one person in this entire world that cannot betray your truth, your trust and your passion, and that is you.

My friend, that is the answer, but I want to finish it up with this. I know that my medium has got you doing this new meditation where you are just enveloped in the light and you see nothing but light all the way around you. You can't see any people or any buildings or anything. You know what he is doing to you, don't you? He is putting you inside your own truth. Yes, when you are in your own truth, that is what it looks like. There is nothing there until you create it. So when you step over that line, you step over into the full truth that the Creator exists in the All That Is. And when you step over that line, you will never ever look back.

Soul Family Relationships

We have a question from someone in the (Internet) chat room. She says, "Can you address the question of whether or not some relationships are chosen before birth for a specific reason? For example, parents or even later, with a mate?"

KIRAEL: Oh, they most assuredly are. To be quite candid with you, most of you will travel in what we call a "soul family." You may get scattered about in different lifetimes, but eventually, most of the soul families will come back together, like now, when it is time for the Shift. When Jesus was on the Earth plane, it was supposed to be the Shift, so many of the families came together at that time.

Oftentimes, when you incarnate into the Earth plane to venture, to learn, to be excited, and to have a great time, many members of the same soul family will choose to be in the same vicinity. They may not choose to be relatives. They may choose to be the person on the bus sitting next to you tomorrow to share one word with you. Then again, they may choose to spend a whole lifetime with you. They may be your brother, your sister, your mother, your father, your husband, or your wife.

You will choose your human family from other energies of your same soul family. Now, you have to get out of your third-dimensional thinking just a wee bit to understand what I am about to say. Your soul family is existent in all Essence Light that is in an evolutionary state of awareness. It then breaks down into gatherings of energies that are of like lessons. Those similar lessons become the lessons of the family, and then energies begin to incarnate. Some of the same soul family often follow each other very closely into the human world.

I will give you an example. There is a couple sitting over here to my left. For this couple, this is a soul journey. Both of them are of the same soul family, but in this lifetime they have reversed roles from previous lifetimes together. We had a dickens of a time getting those two in the same space!

The angels had to overwork themselves with you two. [addressing the couple] When you get home, you just wait. Master Jesus will want to chat with both of you! Now, the person who made the question might see this beautiful couple here and say, "What are these two people doing together?" The answer is that they made this commitment long before they entered into this lifetime. They are doing a life journey, and I might add, they are doing a beautiful job of it.

Now here is another thing. You may make a commitment in your soul family to come here and experience divorce, so someone of your same soul family may come in to help you out with that. They may come here because they love you so much. Do you hear what I am saying? They love you so much that they will come and get divorced from you. Can you imagine the pain of thinking that that is what you are coming here to do? Yet, they will do it for you. And then you wind up hating the person that you divorced for the rest of this incarnation, when the truth is the divorce was born in love. It is amazing, isn't it?

Let's take another question from the next person in line. You seem to be enjoying yourself way too much.

Truth Between Parents and Children

I am learning about expressing the truth of my feelings in the moment, and I am having a difficult time with it. Sometimes it seems that when I am speaking my truth in the moment it hurts another person. How do I know when to shut my mouth and still stay in my truth? How do I know when to express and when not to? You see, all this is new to me—expressing my feelings in the moment.

KIRAEL: If you are going to say something and it is going to hurt someone, then likely you are not in truth.

But I don't know that I am going to hurt that person until I get his or her reaction, and it is like, Wow!

KIRAEL: Then, likely they are having so much trouble with truth that you probably shouldn't be around them. Now let's suppose you can't get away from them.

Let's say it is my son.

KIRAEL: Let's say it is your son. I figured we would get there. See how truth works? Isn't it beautiful? Anyway, let's say it is your son. Here, I will give you an example. Walk up to the microphone and say, "Kirael, I want to ask you a question about something going on between me and my son." You say, "I wanted to do that, but I didn't want everybody to be bored with my question, so I tried to enhance it." Caught you, didn't we?

Sure did.

KIRAEL: So the truth is, you wanted to come up and see if there is some way you can make the blending between you and your son a wee better. The truth is, my friend, that you are not using truth; you are using a "kind of" truth, or words that you think he wants to hear. Therefore, you are not really in your truth; you are in his truth. And then you find out that he doesn't have any truth because his isn't yours, so you wind up with no truth whatsoever.

Here is the easiest truth that I know: You can start by saying, "Here is how I feel, young son," and then you tell the truth—not what you think he wants to hear, but the truth about what you feel. You might say, "I feel scared that you are going to do something that is going to hurt you. And because I love you so much, I am silly enough to worry about that; therefore, I am going to continue to worry. I don't expect you to worry for me, but let's find out what I am worried about." And in this way you go to truth.

So you see, most people in general—I am not talking directly to you at this point—most parents are anything but truthful with their children. Do you know why? Because their parents weren't very truthful with them! You say, "Well, that is not nice. Don't be picking on my parents, Kirael." Well, I don't care; I am picking on them. Parents can be quite untruthful with their children. The children say, "How come I can't ride on the hood of the car?" You say, "Because the police are going to arrest me," but that is not the truth. The truth is, "It is because you are going to splatter all over the glass thing there." You see what I am saying?

Or the children come to you and say, "How come I can't stay out past me curfew?" So you say, "Because it is not acceptable by society's standards." That is not the truth either. Society doesn't give a damn. Oh, I said "damn." Sorry. But here is the truth. "You can't stay out past curfew because I darn well said you can't. And that is one you've got to live with." Then they say, "Oh, all right."

Now what you have really said to them is, "It is because we have got to learn that there are certain things in life that we have to work within in order to make the other things work. And one of the things is understanding that for whatever reason, you chose me as your parent. You chose me as your parent because you had faith that I would use my best guidance to bring you to a point of fulfillment where you could go out and become the guide. That is why you picked me. You didn't pick me just to be your friend. You picked me because you had faith, because you knew that one day you would be a child, a teenager, and you knew that sometimes children don't use the full deductive reasoning that is necessary to understand love. So you picked me because you knew I would stand on your wee shoulders right here and say, 'That is your curfew and you are going to live with it.'"

And I will tell you more. That young child might say, "Oh, all right. It doesn't make a lot of sense. But it makes more sense than if you said I would turn into boogie man or get a pimple on my face if I didn't obey." You know what I mean? This is the kind of truth I am speaking about.

So when you think that you have spoken in truth, but you have just hurt somebody with it, you need to look at your truth. It likely wasn't, because, you see, in order for you to make a truth that is going to hurt somebody, it is likely that you have judged them as incapable of understanding the real truth. And when you make the judgment that they are incapable of understanding real truth, you have just done an injustice. This is because you had not enough faith in yourself to purvey the light of the truth as it is. Work on that one; it will become clear as a bell to you.

A Family's Healing Journey

When my mother experienced a stroke, she provided a gift to the family by opening up a whole new journey of healing. And now we are kind of astounded at the things that she is saying. She is being very truthful and sometimes it is kind of abrasive. What is happening?

KIRAEL: Good question. Let's say that your mom experienced a stroke, and now she is changed, and in your humble judgment she is abrasive. Who is really being abrasive here? Not her; you are, and those people around you are. You see, they are the ones that have got to work with this new situation.

First of all, your mother received a giant *splinter* from her higher self. I mean, a giant splinter. What she had done was use her old splinter for much, much longer than it needed be used. She had patterned her splinter to take care of her young ones, her husband, the home, and all of those things. So at a certain point, she just literally burnt that splinter out, and no longer could that splinter be helpful in the processes that she wanted to learn. [For more on Splinters and Aspects of the Higher Self, see Chapter 8.]

This so-called abrasiveness that you are seeing is just simply the little girl who for years has played this modified role and all of the sudden says, "I'm not playing anymore." So now, all of the so-called "abrased" ones around her are going to have to learn to love what she has become. You say, "Well, that's not fair, Kirael. We want to change her back to what she was." Just stop it right now! You just let her be. You ask, "Yes, but what if she says something foul?" Well then, you might remind her that on this Earth plane that particular kind of statement is a bit foul. And then love her anyway. But don't tell her that she has got to go back to who she was before.

I don't think she would listen to us anyway.

KIRAEL: No, no, she wouldn't. Lead her out of the woods that she is in. In fact, do you know what woods she is in right now? Right now she is in a space where she is saying, "All right, here is where I have got myself. I've got me a new splinter that doesn't fit my body. I know my body is not working so well, but I am kind of enjoying the living dickens right out of this. I kind of like all of the things that are going on."

You can persuade her through love and light that the next part of her journey is going to be more exciting for her if she wants to do it. Yes, she is the same mom, not a different mom, with just a whole lot more beauty in her.

Unmasking the Self in Relationships

Good evening. I am unmasking. Most of the time I like to think that when I am with people I am the real me. I know I enjoy people more when we have things in common and when I am the real me. But what I have come to find is that when I am around certain people, it is like they look at me like they know me and it doesn't matter what words come out of my mouth. It is as if they really do unmask me, which makes me really uncomfortable.

In fact, I had an experience where it was excruciating. I was with this person and I couldn't figure out why I was so uncomfortable. I thought the person was very intuitive, yet I thought she didn't see the real me and know me, so I just burst out bawling. I wondered if that person saw me as ugly, not beautiful. Finally, what I came to think it meant for me was that most of the time I am the one masking everybody.

KIRAEL: That was a long question, yet I will try my best to make pieces of it work for you.

When one is content with unmasking the self, the first thing you will notice is that person doesn't talk very much. When you are really in your truth and being yourself, you are only here to learn; you are not here to teach and expound. If you are a teacher, then you are forced to be in the role of the teacher. But for the most part, even a good teacher is here to learn, right? So the less you say, the more profound you become. The less you say, the more people have to see you for your truth. So as you begin to unmask, my friend, the beauty or the lack of beauty, in your humble opinion or humble judgment, becomes less and less a tool to work with.

Now comes the truth. What is beauty? Beauty is the vibration that emanates from the soul of the one being looked upon. It is that which you emanate, that which becomes your truth. And the more light you emanate, the more others around you will have trouble with you because you become the light while they are there trying to hold their egos intact. The first thing that happens is your light begins to distill their ego system, and then they must run screaming in fear.

The next part of your question is even better, the part where I believe you said that you end up in a massive state of blubbering and bawling. Those of you who cry quite easily must realize something: When you are crying in truth, and not crying to be heard, you have discovered your emotional awareness. Your emotional awareness is the embodiment presence that is closest to your physical world and understandable by your functioning brain. A functioning brain, in the illusionary world of this place called Earth, is what sets up the interaction between energy patterns. So as you unmask yourself, you no longer have the ability to see whether somebody likes what they see or not. You must only continue to unmask your own energy. Otherwise, the moment that you are concerned with how one sees you in your unmasked state is the moment when you have just re-masked yourself. When you disallow that sensation, when you release that judgment, you will find yourself crying a lot. At the same time, you will discover that as you are crying, the world opens you to a different light. Why do you think that you often feel really good after you have had yourself a good cry? It is because the world has begun to open its light to you.

Therefore, the best answer I can offer you concerning your question is this: If you want to go through life unmasked, be prepared for the people around you not to understand, because you are going to be part of a serious minority. Maybe we will change it one day. What do you think?

Death Can Be a Gift in a Relationship

Earlier in the evening, you were talking about a person who may divorce you out of love, through prior agreements. Would you say the same about death?

KIRAEL: Oh, most assuredly. Take a couple of people in a married relationship, for example. It is likely that both have made commitments to be the teacher to each other. In the same way, both have also committed to be the student. And the roles go back and forth in delineating who is in what position at a particular time. But the truth is, my friends, as the Third Dimension comes to closure and you no longer accept duality, meaning one teacher and one student, you come into a place of love where the teacher/student roles do not exist. In that place, only learning exists. Then you will understand why one particular partner may choose to die in a relationship. What a gift that person gives to the partner! What you do with the gift after that is solely up to you. The partner who dies has no energy on it whatsoever.

I can make everybody really upset here by telling you that there is not a single soul leaving Earth who looks back and goes, "Oh, boy, I wish I hadn't left them alone like that." Or, "Gee, I wish I hadn't done that because they look so sad without me." Not one solitary soul evolves and looks back and goes, "Darn, I wish I hadn't done it that way." Not one single solitary soul, my friend, commiserates with you when you are all standing over there during the funeral process boo-hooing and thinking, "Boy, I bet he is just so sad he is not here and he has left us behind." No. He is sitting up on top of the casket with a smile on his face from ear to ear saying, "My God, did I get me some good lessons in this lifetime. Good luck on yours." And then he is out of here.

You say, "Kirael, that sounds very crude." It is not, my friend. When you leave this plane, celebrations begin that you cannot even begin to fathom. The first thing you do is get enveloped in the Light of the Christ energy. That is my favorite time. I can't think of one person that hasn't gone over there and said to me, "Kirael, you weren't kidding! Christ never did leave Earth. He never did!" No, he didn't. When you recognize that the death process is the reality of evolving from one level of consciousness to another level of consciousness, then there is nothing to be afraid of.

My friend, in response to your question: You can be sure that many entities enter into this Earth plane where one has already chosen to do the death experience for the other one, and half the time the other one never appreciates it. In fact, they hold it against them until they get home, at which time they say, "Oh, wow, that was really nice of you. Thank you." There are those out there who would think that Master Kirael takes a terribly light look at the world. When you discover your world is worth looking at lightly, then you will understand.

My Truth, Your Truth

There have been many times when I have felt like I was in my truth in my interactions with different people and in different relationships. I have also felt like the persons I was dealing with were also in their truth, but we still had conflict. Is that because each of us has our own truth?

KIRAEL: I will give you two answers. The first answer is "resonant level truth," which means that when you both feel as though you are in your truth, the only question is, Do I know I am in truth? If you ask yourself, "Do I know I am in truth?" you are likely not in truth.

I mean, I know I was in my truth. I also know that they felt they were in their truth as well, and they most likely were. I am not speaking of one instance, but of a number of different instances throughout my life where things have happened like this, and still continue to happen. Nevertheless, I kind of think—or I know—I was in my truth, and I know that they were in theirs. But aren't both truths true for each individual?

KIRAEL: Yes. Be clear with that, my friend. Be clear that a truth is on the level of your own awareness. It must come from the core of your own essence. Be also clear that your level of awareness may differ from the interactive essence of the other person. I say "interactive essence" because that essence has chosen to interact in your reality, but you are in the space of illusion control. In this space, you are allowing the other's essence to be in truth to a point of truth that will measure to your point of truth. Therefore, the truth of knowingness is a scale of understanding. And as long as you are measuring truth on that scale, the level of vibration is the set point at which you will discover the light vibration, wherein it will hold itself in a space that is understandable for you. But because you hold the limited 10% conscious awareness of the human brain within the illusion of time as a truth, that truth has the delineable energy to move itself from one moment to the next without creating a span of vibrational illusion in between.

So in the process of bringing these two spans into oneness, your level of truth oftentimes will not match the truth of another evolving entity, yet both of you can be in your own truth at the same time. The only way past that is through the light of recognition in the All That Is.

You are the Entertainment

I have a question about the relationship that we have with entertainment. In order for us to stay in the Third Dimension, it seems to me that the biggest problem is the breakdown of entertainment. Essentially we have more movies, more Internet, which is all the same. Everything seems to be exploding in whole new tiers of meaninglessness, and now the whole planet seems to be waking up, but it doesn't wake up. So, of course, we are finding ourselves more entertainment. How do we sort that out in the moment—I know it is through a meditative process—but what is the subliminal event that cuts through this and illuminates entertainment as the drug that all of us seem to be addicted to?

KIRAEL: First of all, I want to say, "Welcome to the Third Dimension," because that is what it is all about. If there was one creative, shall I say, "10-step program" that you could take, it would be to discover that you don't exist.

Now I want to clarify that because I don't like to leave my friends up in the air.

In reality, the truth you would discover is that you don't exist and that this is just a series of illusionary vibrational patterns. It is a game basically. You are playing the game at whatever level you are capable of playing it. The diversionary tactics that you use to bring out the fullness of the game is entertainment. They are your delusionary processes that hold the captivity of your brain spectrum in the 10% reality.

You mentioned the word *computers*. I give you this as an example: The reason they put games on the computer, such as where you shoot things out of the sky, is to keep you from learning the truth of the computer. They keep those games in there to keep you solidified with your understanding of the Earth plane, right? They make you understand that by shooting things out of the sky you cannot really understand that the computer is a replication of the third-dimensional matrix. When you become clear with that, you will also be aware that somewhere, somebody is really pulling the strings, and the somebody is *you*.

By pulling the strings, you can begin to bring a live event process into a fulfillment space whereby nothing is left to chance. When you have discovered that, you automatically move from this reality anyway. What we from the Guidance Realm are saying by our being here—and you have opened this question for me at a perfect place—is that we enjoy life as much as you do, but without the illusion of all the discontent. Therefore, we don't have to entertain ourselves other than by opening up into our own light, as you so eloquently stated, in the meditative world.

You will come to the clarity in the new reality of the Fourth Journey, or as you call it, the Fourth Dimension, that the only places of truth are found within the world of meditation. And then, when you are through with that truth, you will come back to this form of entertainment, and you will live it out in the entertainment world for you will have discovered that *you* are the entertainment. In truth, you try to look at others as though you aren't.

Closing Statement

My friends, I thank each and every one of you for being here. To my friends in the chat room, thank you so much for joining our energies this evening. Hopefully, we can meet again soon and have even more questions. Until that time, let your relationship be *you*, and then you will discover the truth of relationships with others.

Good evening, my friends.

6 THE FOUR PILLARS OF CONSCIOUS CREATION

Opening Statement

KIRAEL: Good evening.

We would like to venture this evening into something that we call the Four Pillars of Conscious Creation. In the beauty of what is known as prayer, meditation, sleepstate programming and masterminding lies the clarity that you are not alone on this journey into the Earth plane.

For the longest time, there have been those who would like to believe that they walk upon this Earth with no one to watch over them. Yet at the same time, it is found in many of your religious studies that you cannot exist without certain energies smiling down upon you. Thus I offer unto you this message: You can and do have interaction with the entirety of all worlds. You simply need to remember that you have entered into this Earth journey in your own light as a gift from the Creator.

You live in a world controlled by your thoughts, which were first conceived in the Creator's Light. Because your energy is part of the Creator's Light, you have gifted unto yourself this same line of conscious creative thought that will take you from one dimension to the next. The Four Pillars of Conscious Creation are the processes that will take you there by connecting your truth to the All That Is.

At this point in your Earth journey you are awakening to the truth that to be human takes you beyond what you were taught in school. Have you ever considered yourselves "upright, two-brained, mid-air breathers?" Let me clarify that to prevent your brain from going into overload. Humans are classified as "two-brained" because your brain comes in two lobes: one, which you consider the 10% portion, and the other, the 90% portion of the brain.

You are considered a "mid-air breather" because you in the human world don't succeed very well at breathing underwater. (You don't seem to breathe well in the etheric fabric either.) "Upright" because you are a species that walks on two legs. Thus, we view you as "upright, two-brained, mid-air breathers." This description changes as you begin to practice and understand that the Four Pillars of Conscious Creation are your only way out of this dimension of duality.

When we talk about these Pillars of Conscious Creation, we are talking about connecting with the world beyond the human reality—a world much larger and much more detailed than yours. I am referring to worlds invisible to your physical eye which exist as part of the Creation of All Light. It is time that you understand *you are never alone*; you are the part of the Creator's Light experiencing life on a dimension quite unusual for the Creator's energy. I mean "unusual" in that there are human confines and constrictions that you utilize to inspire yourself to do a journey that is beyond most.

In essence, we of the guidance world, the angelic reality, and all realities between, are envious of your human journey. You can have experiences that we have long lost. For instance, the last time many of us picked up a golden goblet of wine was centuries over centuries ago. Yet the vast majority of us who have had the honor of working through the creative space of Earth still have fond memories of the things that you experience. Hence, we have our parts to play in this journey of Conscious Creation and it is time that you understand your part. The way to do this is by living these Pillars to the fullest. I assure you that once you establish them as Four Pillars in your life, your life begins anew.

I might forewarn you that once you begin this journey, you cannot, and will not, return to being the same human you were before. Once you fully embrace these principles, you will raise your energies well above the normal human world. It is not to say that the Four Pillars will make you more money or give you better relationships. Though they may, it is more about discovering the potential already within you.

What is your potential? You are God Light incarnate, my friends. This means that there are no restrictions on you other than those you place upon yourself. Living the Four Pillars dispels those barriers and you find yourself entering worlds that you only dreamed of before. The gaps that you once perceived between you and the angelic forces and the guidance world are nonexistent. I say "nonexistent" because your minds are not yet capable of deciphering a nonexistent being such as yourself, for you experience your world on Earth through the five-sensory abilities. For instance, in your sleepstate, when you move out of the 10% mind, we are able to travel together to other worlds. So as you awaken the fullness—and I emphasize—the *fullness* of the Four Pillars of Conscious Creation, you are free to do as you would with no limitations upon you. You gain the totality of experience and free the 10% mind to open to your 90% consciousness.

Once you begin to use the Four Pillars, you will begin to awaken your sixth sense. You cannot go in search of the sixth sense; your sixth sense *is* you. The five senses that you identify yourself as are but an aspect of you, while the sixth sense is your truth. It is the part of you that carries your original will or purpose for being on the Earth journey.

The definition of the human reality must be one word only, and that word is *illusionary*. It is your thoughts, your will and your words collectively that draw a significant amount of vibrational magnetic force to hold together a world as you perceive it through your eyes. When you have accomplished the fullness of the Four Pillars of Conscious Creation, you will move from one dimension to the next by thought processing alone.

As long as you regard yourselves as third-dimensional beings restrained by the five senses, your lives are limited. When you come to the clarity that you *are* a manifestation, then manifesting anything in your life will be absolute. You will have no limitations placed upon you then. For example, if all of you sitting in this circle this day came to the complete collective consciousness that you would all disappear from this room, you would all disappear. Yet if one of you remained weakened in this belief system, then no one would leave. Hence, the world plane as you know it in collective consciousness exists because you believe what you see.

Now this may be the most important thing I say this evening: through the Four Pillars you will move with a will—an intent—that is best aligned with the journey that you planned for this dimension. You won't be limited. Instead, you will live that journey exactly as you perceived you would. And here is the best part: you can now take the problems and the perceived limitations that you acquired over years through thought, and you may discard them, opening your life to a much higher vibration of experience.

You will eventually want to share this with all of your friends, but for now, those of you who collectively bring your consciousness to the will of the sixth sense understand that your limitations have been exhausted. From being a "two-brained, mid-air breather," you are becoming "one-brained, mid-air breathers." Having developed your brain through the Four Pillars, your mind no longer needs to be divided into the two brain lobes and thus can immediately move into a one-brain system. Once you have accomplished this, everything within your thought system can be willed into existence. All you need to do then is control your thought system.

In short, my friends, your commitment to the Four Pillars of Conscious Creation is the measure of your willingness to allow yourself the right to move into your truth. Whilst you grow in your understanding of the angels and the guides and those of other reality focuses through the Four Pillars, you become the in-lightened of your own species. In that, you shall hold yourself to the light that best suits the Creator's overall plan. Within that light, you shall ease yourself into a more beautiful space that will allow you the journey to be free. Freedom is the success of entering into the Four Pillars of Conscious Creation.

Questions & Answers

First Pillar of Conscious Creation: Prayer

How would you suggest that we pray?

KIRAEL: Pray from your heart. The best prayers are from the human heart. They are prayers of gratitude, recognizing the perfection in all things and our essential oneness with the God Light. Believe me, my friends, prayers of the human heart are aligned to the Light and are therefore listened to without fail. The clearer you are in prayer, the more we the guides and angels can do. Indeed, you can become so clear that it would seem that we did it for you. Understand that there is no separation between us, for in truth, we act together to get it done.

Mantra Prayers

It is interesting how we humans were taught the words to use in prayer. Were those words programmed?

KIRAEL: Of course they were. Even the beautiful words of Master Jesus, the so-called "Lord's Prayer," were turned into a kind of mantra to be repeated again and again without much understanding. The prayer itself is beautifully done, but as you suggest, many other prayers simply perpetuate the mastermind of control.

Let Your Prayers Be Inner-Directed

What suggestions do you have for people who are just beginning to formulate their own prayers to open up a dialogue with the unseen forces of light? What can they do instead of the traditional mantra prayers, as you call them?

KIRAEL: Stop thinking! Mantra prayers train you to think that you are limited. This is the truth. They keep you believing that the forces seemingly beyond your reality will have little to do with you. When you stop thinking and allow your 90% mind to take over, the will of your inner core guidance then manifests itself in words, and the words themselves guide you in prayer. Like automatic writing, maybe we should call it "automatic praying." When you allow your heartfelt desires to become the reality focus of a vibrational pattern, the words flow. The prayers become inner-directed by the will of your higher presence or by your sixth, intuitive sense.

Once your prayers are in that flow, everything that you say from there forward is picked up in the etheric light. The etheric light factor then aligns the processes to move to the will of your words. This means that once you are clear on what you are praying for and you allow the will of your higher self to guide the prayer, there is absolutely nothing that can stand in the way of that will. That will is of Creation itself. Hence, your prayer is automatically aligned to the will and the words that you use. And in that energy your prayer flows out into the universe, where it does not know time or space, beginning or end. It only knows to gather the forces that the prayer has called for.

It is sometimes very difficult for you to recognize that your journey is but a focus of energy. Thus, when you remove your ego from the process of the prayer, your prayer has the freedom to disperse its own energy. When your prayer is clearly worded and focused, the will of the word takes over. The energy finds its way into a directed beam of light that will search every nook and cranny of this Earth plane to bring forth the answers. It will align the answers to your prayers with your path, and believe me, my friends, you will literally have to trip and break a leg to keep it from happening. That is the way your world works.

By inviting the guidance factors to pick up on the energy of your prayer, you open yourself to the oneness of the 100% mind. If you are operating at 10% of your mind's capacity, you have a 10% chance of pulling the whole process together. If you are operating at 20% or at 90%, you can see a grand difference. Believe me, prayer from the heart is an automatic focus. It is the beam, the thread, which runs through your universe gathering whatever your light desires. Remember, this energy knows no end.

So when you pray, bring the focus of the Creator I AM into your prayer, and when you do, the I AM searches out what you are praying for beyond time and space. The human world says, "I am the I AM presence." The words, "I AM Presence" is the Creator. The God Creator is the infinite I AM. Yet if you are human—and please find the humor in this—when you say *I am*, you are automatically *I was*!

Play with prayer if you like, my friends. Use mantras if you wish. At the same time, remember that the prayers that come from your heart, the prayers that you create in the I AM are the ones that will endlessly search out the answers to your prayers. The clearer you make your prayers, the more easily they move beyond the noisy thought systems of the human mind. That is prayer in its most defined, divine process.

A Step and a Prayer

I have heard that when all is said and done, everything is prayer. Could you comment on that?

KIRAEL: I will be most thrilled to do so. The reason I say that, my friend, is because there is no end. The end is the beginning. First, understand that your life on Earth was part of a prophecy laid out long before years could be measured. The prophecy of which I speak was designed by beings of light giving you parallel lines to follow. Along these parallel lines, a matrix was created. This matrix was the human experience.

It is not a play on words when I say "the end is the beginning." The end which you look for is the end times of the prophecy that you are currently experiencing. At the same time, this prophecy has already ended in some fashion. Hence, you are now playing out what has already become the beginning.

At this stage, prayer must guide your every movement. You will not step one foot before the other without stopping long enough to pray. Pray to align each step of your journey. Make it the most exhilarating experience possible.

The Answer to Prayer is in the Question

I often find that when I pray with passion I am very centered and clear on what I am praying for. At times I am so clear that I receive my answers during my prayer. Can you elaborate on that?

KIRAEL: In order for your brain to formulate a question, you must have the answer. Because you live in a duality system based on a prophecy, all things function as duality sequencing. This means that for you to say "yes," you must know what "no" means. Therefore, to ask a quesion, you must already have the answer. So when you enter into prayer, your prayer thought is actually divided, and one thought segment singularly imposes upon itself the visual experience of what you wish to understand. This seemingly gives you the answer to your prayer.

In other words, you create a prayer through the will and you clarify that prayer by putting words to it. When you reach a point of clarity during your prayer, you reframe and reflect. You literally bend the energy to reflect the answer that you already have. Hence, it seems as though you had the answer before you began to pray. In fact, you did have the answer, but you didn't remember it. In essence, your mind creates a space in your memory where it can unfold before you, and then it feels like you just understood it. Sometimes it is called *déjà vu*. It is as though a mirror of the question you asked reflects back upon you the answer that you knew before asking the question.

Manifesting Prayers of Gratitude

You have said that the most powerful form of prayer is the prayer of gratitude, reinforcing the notion that everything is in perfection. So in a prayer of gratitude, someone might say, "Thank you, God, for sending me my divine soul mate," while in reality not having had a date in 10 years. It stretches the human mind to say "thank you" for something that you don't already have. Could you explain how a prayer of gratitude works?

KIRAEL: Let's use the example you have given. Let's say that you have been mate-free for ten years and at the same time have been praying in gratitude for that future mate. In truth, your mate has been standing within arm's length of you all that time. It is only that you have not succeeded in manifesting your mate into this dimension.

My friend, you are being given everything. Your gratitude is already being honored. If you are praying from the level of Truth, Trust, and Passion, it is already taking place. In the Third Dimension, which you currently reside in (or which you feel that you currently reside in), it is your higher self's responsibility to allow you to do the journey to bring your prayers to fulfillment. And while the higher self will not allow that perfect mate to manifest itself before you until you reach that point of clarity, he or she has already been created.

Along those same lines, I am telling you in the light of truth that when you are lying in your bed praying for some money to be yours, it is already yours. The money cannot manifest, however, because you believe in the "two-brained theory" and allow your 10% brain to persuade you that the money is not yours. When you become "one-brained"—that is, when you use the Four Pillars of Conscious Creation at their fullest force—the money will appear. Money, a mate, whatever you wish will manifest within an alignment that best suits your needs at that stage of your evolutionary journey.

And the manifestation of your prayer comes with the fullness of its own creation. Here is an example that may challenge you, but let's try. If one day you were sitting at a bus stop praying for your mate to come into your life, and a person sat down next to you and if you thought, "He is just like the person I was thinking about," *he would be the one.* You would probably wonder if this person had been living a life before he or she appeared before you, and the answer is no. But now, in creation, this person has a light to offer you. He or she would even have a history of places lived, of people known—indeed, all of the history deemed necessary for a human to have.

One of you in this room may be from that dimension. Indeed, all of you may be from that dimension. You may have all come because I prayed you here! Yet, you all have histories; you all have the fullness of creation that it takes to be a reality focus.

Let me add to that because I still hear questions in your mind. To pray in gratitude for the abundance and success that you have created in your life is to utilize the Four Pillars of Conscious Creation in the most simplistic way. The Four Pillars—prayer, meditation, sleepstate programming, and masterminding—need to become the full focus of your energy force to make your world become a so-called reality. Practicing them allows you to understand that you are illusionary, that everything you create is illusionary, and that it is *that* simple to create your own reality. Your words, your creations of abundance, your creations of gratitude are heard throughout all linear forces of light. And as with prayers themselves, they begin to align everything to make it happen in your life. All you need to do then is vibrate it into existence.

That is about a four-hour dissertation I have just condensed into three minutes.

Second Pillar of Conscious Creation: Meditation

How do you define meditation?

KIRAEL: I would define *meditation as the conscious awareness of the vibrational spectrums within which light can pulsate.* When you are in deep forms of what you consider to be meditation, you are literally in control of the light particles that will be utilized through thought manifestation. Through meditation you define how you would like the particles arranged. Then depending upon your vibratory structure and your belief systems, you create the appropriate reality in the Third Dimension.

For example, if you are working on the process of abundance but you have a fear of abundance—which is common on your Earth plane—your meditative state aligns these light particles and places them into your conscious awareness. From there, you draw the particles from mass consciousness, on through the shields of your ego, so to speak, and into your reality. However, if there is any fear and if the ego is strong, you automatically set up a pattern of energy preventing the abundance from manifesting.

You see, particle light is malleable. You can create anything you can conceivably think of. You are only limited by what you hold in human thought, yet in meditation you can release human thought. When you do that, you find yourself within the same particle value streams from which all life began. You are then at the very beginning of all life essence.

Within a meditative state is found the possibility to fulfill all that you need for your life journey. Your meditative state is your truth. It is your particle light, what you are made of. In meditation, you find your wholeness, your collective consciousness of all reality forces.

You are a Meditation

I have also heard that every moment in life can be a state of meditation. How does that relate to meditation and prayer?

KIRAEL: I think you will find a bit of a smile cross your face as you hear my answer.

It has been said that every moment is the foundation of a meditation because your higher self remains in a state of meditation as it allows you to experience the Earth reality. In essence, you are on Earth clocking time while your higher self has only to sit in meditation, allowing you to experience all of the different potentials and possibilities. Hence, on another level you are a light particle being of sound vibration in a meditative state. What you have been told is absolute truth: you are a meditation.

Phases of Meditation

Do we communicate with our higher selves and other nonphysical reality forces during meditation?

KIRAEL: You are always in contact with your higher self; you just don't remember. When you are in meditation, the first few minutes are spent drifting back and forth between realities. You open yourself to information being downloaded into your system in this phase of meditation. The second phase takes you within the core of meditation, where you drift in and out of different realities, much like during your sleepstate. At this deeper level you literally interact with your brothers and sisters of other light sources. They also work closely with your higher self, offering guidance on how to interact with them on more intricate levels.

Meditation is much like going to school. You have the pre-school or going into meditation to have fun with it. Here you can journey into different parts of the more recognizable planes of light. Then you have the core essence level of meditation, where you are schooled in the wisdom of other reality forces. Finally, you have what we call the graduation level, where you take that information, and with your higher self and all guidance realities, you practice discerning which information to bring back with you to this dimension.

Meditation and the Four Energetic Bodies

You have consistently brought forth the importance of meditation and now, more than ever, as the Shift accelerates, those who practice meditation will see the Shift in its truth. Will you share with the human world what happens to the physical, mental, emotional and spiritual bodies of an entity when he or she participates in the practice of meditation?

KIRAEL: In the world of meditation a number of things occur. The first is the thought of meditation itself. With just the thought, meditation begins to adjust the physical and spiritual portions of your body and links them together. On the physical level, when one achieves the desired level of one's meditation (whatever that level might be), the brain itself begins to re-circuit its energy. In essence, the lower vibrating 10% part of your conscious mind begins to diminish its activity, and the circuitry starts to evolve its energy into the wiser, more expansive 90% portion. This is why you lose track of time during meditation because time only exists in the 10% mind. What really occurs in this re-wiring of the brain is a profound shifting of energy. An actual portal between the 90% mind and the 10% mind presents itself, thereby moving into the one-brain potential.

The next physical thing to take place is that the body itself, not the brain, begins to vibrate at a cellular level, thereby expanding the mirrors between the cells to an in-lightened state. As they expand their energies, more light penetrates the physical body, allowing healing to take place at a quicker rate.

At the same time, in what we call the emotional body, the emotions themselves begin to diminish their usual ups and downs, and actually move towards a balanced space. The emotions are drawn from the physical plane into an etheric alignment, where these feelings exert less and less influence on the thinking process.

Next, the mental world begins to operate on a level beyond our usual grasp of third-dimensional reality. The mental level searches within itself for questions that have arisen since the last meditation. It answers them in such a fashion that your mind begins to absorb this process, for the mental world does not exist in your mind; it lives in your spirit. Once it has recognized the questions that you have searched for, it aligns with what are called the *Akashic Records of Answers*, and meditation allows access to those records.

In the spiritual body, the very thought of meditation begins to enhance the spiritual awareness of the individual. You awaken to the truth that you are not your physical body. You become more aware of your truth—that you are of spirit. And what you see from your spirit self in meditation is the reflection of love. So in the spiritual world you will find an opening that creates an expansion of light not available in the physical. There are no limitations in the spiritual world.

Meditation is far more than closing your eyes and going into a state of unconsciousness. Rather, you enter a state of enhanced consciousness in which avenues are opened to understanding who you truly are.

In Meditation You are Not Human

People new to meditation often say they have difficulty meditating for more than 5 or 10 minutes at a time. Any longer than that, they find their thoughts intrude, and they have trouble focusing inward. Do you have any words of advice for them?

KIRAEL: Yes. *Stop pretending that you are human.* That may sound outrageous, but it is probably one of the most truthful statements I can make. When you enter into meditation, your sole goal should be to realize that you are spirit; that you are not a human being, but that you are spirit *be-ing* a human. The reason people find themselves twitching and bouncing about is because of the fear of knowing that the human part of them is not as real as they think it is.

Another point needs to be made about the historical mastermind opposing the practice of meditation. If you look closely at many of your scriptures and your books of old, you will find that it has been in the interests of existing power structures to control both the outflow and inflow of information. From this perspective, it may be easier to understand why meditation has not been encouraged. In meditation you discover that you have access to information otherwise unavailable to the human population. As a result, it was instilled in the populace long ago that meditation was somehow afoul of "divine" law, and therefore not to be practiced. In truth, the God Light law is each of you could spend much more time in meditation than you do now.

Why Prayer, Not Meditation, in Religion

In your book, "Kirael Volume II: The Genesis Matrix," you spoke about the structure of religion as practiced in formalized religions. You pointed out that the church powers wanted people to pray, but not to meditate. Can you comment on that?

KIRAEL: Praying is a statement of what you desire. Prayer, in a manner of speaking, is you, the Earth human, talking to God, or the unseen powers. Meditation, on the other hand, can be seen as God, or the unseen powers, talking to you.

People have been led to believe that in prayer only the chosen or appointed few could interact directly with the God Source. Many of the prayers found in your great books of wisdom, even the one known as "The Lord's Prayer," were changed by those who would deter you from thinking above the level of thought of the leaders of the day. Prayer was encouraged by those in control because it kept you confined to the illusion that you are only human. Prayers spoken aloud were encouraged, yet words themselves can be a limitation. Words are, in fact, a limitation experienced only by humans. Meditation, on the other hand, releases you from the limitations imposed by society, a society based on control. It reveals the truth of who and what you are—a divine aspect of the All That Is, from which you are never separate.

There is No Bad Meditation

Of all the forms and varieties of meditation—mantra meditation, contemplative meditation, guided meditation, counting the breath, assuming certain postures and mudras, and so on—is there something you would specifically recommend or say to the beginner?

KIRAEL: I would say "Congratulations, because you are meditating."

bad meditation. The closest you can get to a bad meditation is n at all. The simple washing of lettuce, taking a walk, or hugging ___ ___ ___ forms of meditation. Indeed, your waking state is a form of meditation.

Everyone seems to want to search for another person's answer whilst trying to find their own. Once you understand that the diverse forms and levels of meditation exist only to pacify the human mind, you recognize that whatever level chosen is the perfect level at the time—even the twitching and bouncing about. What I suggest to you is this: Your intent will lead you faster than anything else that can be taught to you in human verbiage or in different meditative styles. Your intent alone can bypass all the self-imposed limitations that you experience. It is not so much technique or the length of time one practices; what matters is the clear intent of what is sought through meditation.

Going Beyond Fears with Meditational Music

You have spoken about the "powers that be" making it difficult to meditate by creating a mastermind of fear. Since fear is a vibrational energy, would the use of music dissipate the fear, thereby allowing people to more easily experience the state of grace, the sense of oneness, in meditation?

KIRAEL: Indeed, it would. What music does, as does Signature Cell Healing©, is it actually touches the body system. The sounds of the music and the beat of the music create a vibrational wave that literally engages and touches the physical body.

The physical system is the most susceptible to the vibration of touch. It does not necessarily entail the touch of another human, but the actual passing of energy through the system. Music creates a wave of energy that enters into the cellular awareness, causing each cell to vibrate. The cellular structures thus begin to in-lighten themselves by having a more expanded awareness of their own light, which is then projected throughout the physicality of the human experience. Soft, mellow music, for example, will naturally create an inner relaxation not always recognized by the busy little third-dimensional mind. By combining music and meditation with a set intent on what you wish to experience, the telomeres of your DNA can release a vibrational energy that allows you to go beyond the usual self-imposed limitations. With this combination of music, meditation, and intent, you may literally open a doorway through which to experience oneness within yourself and with Creation. [Signature Cell Healing© is a form of energetic healing practiced at the Honolulu Church of Light]

A Guided Meditation with Kirael

Could you give us an example of how one might achieve this sense of oneness in meditation?

KIRAEL: It would be my pleasure.

First, be still for a moment and draw in some deep prana breaths. Next, I would like each of you in your own mind's eye to draw a vision of the Master Jesus, or the Master Buddha, or the Lord Krishna. Visualize him standing five feet in front of you. See him in whatever shape or form you might imagine, and notice that as you look upon him, he seems to glow. See a soft glow emanating from his body and feel the glow from a distance of five feet. Feel it as it wraps around you and holds you, as though you are wrapped in a soft baby's blanket. You may find yourself experiencing shifts in your body: your breathing slowing down, or perhaps tears welling up in your eyes. Just let yourself feel the presence of the Light. Then, ever so slowly, begin to merge with the Light. As it approaches slowly, you are overwhelmed with love.

Within a split second, the Light merges with your light. You feel the Light within your legs, your arms, your body. But most of all, you feel it in the core of your heart. It is as though your body couldn't move if it had to. Your body wants only to experience this gift of Light, in every cell and fiber of its being.

Let yourself feel the Light fully now, as you begin to understand that all the energy surrounding you now is the Creator. You and the Light have merged within Creation, until you can see nothing but white light. In this is the experience of beauty, my friends, when one sees with the eyes of the Christ Consciousness. And remember that each of you is the Christ; each of you is the Buddha, for each of you is that Light. Now, slowly return to this reality, while remaining within the beauty of that Light.

What you have just experienced is the truth that no one can return to the Creator but by passing through the Light of Christ. The simple truth is: *You are the Light of Christ.*

Third Pillar of Conscious Creation: Sleepstate Programming

Can you explain the process of sleepstate programming?

KIRAEL: Sleepstate programming will be addressed thusly: You are a magnetic society, meaning that your vibratory systems exist within a matrix of energy that bases itself on magnetic structure. Your entire world is held together by the formation of what we call "intent particle-ization." When you form the intent to communicate with someone's higher self in a sleepstate program, you are directing your higher self to enter this matrix of energy to search throughout the etheric fabric for all vibrations congruent with your intent. In the process of sleepstate programming, you begin to remove the filters from your reality. Then you can see that you have a connected status, a latticework interlacing the etheric energies that each and every one of you taps into. You travel in this etheric light on a constant basis. It is called the etheric fabric and is very much attainable, very much understandable.

When you take sleepstate programming in total seriousness, you will see the endless routes you can take within the intermeshing network of the etheric fabric surrounding your Earth. You can send your energies into this beautiful network of thought patterns, and much like sonar is used here on the Earth plane, your thought energies will search out the higher selves of the people you desire to reach. Your thought energies will continue in this manner until you have gathered enough energy to find your way into their reality, first through their 90% consciousness, and then through the portals of their 10% minds.

Your Higher Self May Intervene

When we ask our higher self to communicate with another person's higher self in sleepstate programming, are we intruding upon that other person and violating his space?

KIRAEL: Your sleepstate programming will be tested in the etheric fabric by your higher self as to whether or not it is of the Light. If it is being sent out in a selfish fashion, it will have a very difficult time succeeding in the etheric light. The higher self of that individual is also able to decipher and block what is coming towards it, regardless of how much power is placed behind the sleepstate programming. Should you, as Lightworkers, be set upon by outside forces not of the Light, your higher selves will automatically intervene in the etheric energy and shunt that energy into a different space.

Let's suppose that the sleepstate program is being invoked in the highest good for all concerned, but the person initiating the sleepstate program is hoping to have a relationship with a person who is not showing the same interest. The intent may be based in love, but the reality is that the interest is one-sided.

KIRAEL: Then it would not be Light. First of all, the "highest good" does not exist. It is either Light or not Light. The moment there is the slightest gray area, you might as well not waste your time because the higher self of even the darkest energy pattern is always in the protective mode, protecting in the Light.

Partnering with Your Higher Self

In working with our higher selves in sleepstate programming, I have heard you say that at times we must be more assertive with our higher selves and at other times not. How is one to know when to be more assertive or less assertive?

KIRAEL: You will know when you have over-asserted yourself to your higher self when everything around you goes pitch black and you find yourself lying down looking up. [*laughter*] This would signify that your higher self has literally put you in that position to have the chance to restructure and straighten out whatever mess it has made.

The way for the human world to approach the higher self is through prayer. If you are not using prayer to attune to your higher self, I suggest you communicate with your higher self in a delicate manner. Otherwise, you are going to use words that are not willed from the God Source. You are going to use words that you have learned here in this dimension to try and strike a bargain with your higher self, and, believe me, higher selves do not bargain.

As I stated earlier, the higher self is in what you would consider to be a constant meditative state; hence, it recognizes Creation as having no limitations of time and space. So all you need to do is, without great inflection in your voice, take your prayers to the height of clarity about what you are asking the higher self to accomplish with you. And I emphasize *with* you, not *for* you. The higher self then automatically generates its energy into the higher self of whom you wish to work with. It does not have to search the people out, meaning you don't have to instruct your higher self to go to that person.

If, for example, you are in Hawaii and you are working with someone in Germany in a sleepstate program, you do not have to send your higher self to Germany. Making your higher self go around the globe would bore the living daylights out of it. Instead, you can simply inform your higher self of the location of that person. Then, your higher self proceeds to generate its energy into the higher self of that person.

Bring your prayers to the higher self with passion and be impassioned in your sleepstate programming, for your passion, along with clarity of intent, reinforces your desire. In fact, while you are communicating your sleepstate intentions to your higher self, it is simultaneously transmitting them to the higher self of the other person. First, they confer on whether or not you are in truth. Then, they consider your sleepstate program desire.

My friends, if you use sleepstate programming, it will bring clarity and energy to your reality focus, and you will discover that there is nothing out of bounds.

Fourth Pillar of Conscious Creation: Masterminding

What is masterminding? How does it work as energy?

KIRAEL: Masterminding is a process in which two or more are gathered for the purpose of utilizing collective consciousness to consciously create each person's desires. In the process of masterminding, each person first brings his or her thoughts into clear and focused statements of intent. Next, the group collectively brings their statements of intent into one confined space. In turn, the statements are experienced as vibrations of electrical impulses which are transmitted from the physical body. The electrical impulses then catch magnetic waves, seeking out impulses that are congruent with theirs.

How Masterminding Works

Can you give us an example of how masterminding works?

KIRAEL: First, let me define masterminding in another way: *A mastermind is an accumulation of vibrational thought patterns that join with other like vibrations, gathering enough energy to focus itself into manifestation.* That answer may be a bit easier for some to understand.

How does it work? When a group of Lightworkers join together in the same intent to mastermind an outcome, those thought patterns are collectively entered into the etheric fabric. There it joins with other thought particles, one connecting with another and then another, searching through all the universes to find the proper reality focus. Then it expands itself again until it becomes a space in time and is written into the etheric fabric. From there, it finds its way into the 90% consciousness and searches for the portal into the 10%, or third-dimensional consciousness, where it finally manifests. The end result is dependent upon the density of one's ego and the clarity of one's channel.

Creating a Mastermind Group

How do you create a good mastermind group?

KIRAEL: To put it in some perspective, a mastermind group is only as strong as the totality of who you are collectively. Your mastermind group is also as weak as the weakest individual link. Thus, you know you have a good mastermind group when your group is getting what it desires both collectively and individually.

When you create a mastermind, there is absolutely nothing that will stop it unless somebody weakens up a link. So if you are not getting what your mastermind group desires, you need to talk about it at one of your mastermind group meetings. You need to find out how each person is practicing the Four Pillars we are talking about here. When you know this, you will find the weakness in your mastermind group.

A mastermind is not simply two or more people sharing their thoughts. Instead, it is similar to the process of prayer. By intent, your mastermind statement defines a certain particle value that hones itself, seeking out the energy force that you wish to manifest. If the particle light comes up short, it is then up to the mastermind group to create whatever it is you are looking to manifest. I said "create" because, believe me, what you are looking for does not exist. That's right. If you are looking for it, it cannot exist. Hence, the collective energy of the mastermind group is necessary to bring it to a focus in creation. Once it is brought to focus, it now exists. Once it exists, it is yours for the taking by aligning your dimensional factors and manifesting it into your life.

Is it possible to have a mastermind of one that draws other people's energy into it, in essence, creating a mastermind group "in absentia"?

KIRAEL: It is definitely possible. However, you do not achieve the single-pointed clarity you might otherwise achieve in a group that is masterminding together. When you come together with two or more, you move your meandering thoughts and unfocused wishes into clear, focused mastermind statements. This assures a far better end result.

A Regular Practice

Every night I ask my higher self to join the higher selves of people in mastermind groups that I participate in and with other people that I have agreed to meet in the sleepstate. It is a form of ritual. I am wondering if it is necessary for me to do that every night, or can I set it on autopilot?

KIRAEL: It is absolutely not necessary to do it every night—as soon as what you want accomplished is accomplished.

That may be the shortest answer I will give all night.

Masterminding Abundance

It seems that no matter how much money I have in the bank, I am always in the lack mode. How can I mastermind myself into my natural state of abundance?

KIRAEL: There are only a few billion people asking that question today. [*laughter*] You must realize that your thought process is contained in the 10% journey. You have learned to pretend that you are the 10% and that you are human. You have fallen prey to everything the over-mastermind has set for you in such a fashion as to make you feel that you are in lack, no matter how much you have. In this way, you have been striving in the 10% and not spending time in the 90%; hence, you have become controllable by the over-mastermind, also known as the collective fears of the Earth plane.

Now, you must be willing to go beyond what you *think* you know, because if you can think it, it is in the 10%. If you can *know* it, it is in the 90%. One of the hardest tasks is to know that you are wealthy beyond your wildest dreams; that abundance is only a state of consciousness; and that money is a 10% reality focus used by the over-mastermind to maintain its control over the world of the human. You have been controlled through money since the beginning of money. Such is the thickness of your veils.

Free Will and Masterminding

Regarding free will and the process of masterminding, how much is in our control and how much is not? Can we mastermind winning the lottery, for example, or is that determined by either chance or predestiny?

KIRAEL: Everything is in your control. With respect to the lottery, your higher self will know if it is something you are prepared to work with or not. If it is your life quest to win millions of dollars in a lottery, the likelihood is that you will win it, but the truth is that notoriously the younger souls win lotteries. If you can see the devastation that millions of dollars creates for a human being, you will understand that not many higher evolved souls want to be there. Your reference to *predestiny* simply means the manifestation of a thought consciousness that is controlled by the *destiny maker*. You are in total control, and everything is in absolute perfection when it happens.

What about the injunction "not my will but thy will—God's will—be done"?

KIRAEL: Yes, it is absolute truth. But remember, you are God.

Meaning that God's will is my will?

KIRAEL: Yes. When it says in the Lord's prayer, "thy will be done," that *is* your will.

You are the Creator in Masterminding

It seems to me that this whole process of masterminding and creation is a process to know that we are God, that we are the Creator. (Kirael applauds.) Yet, in working through the mastermind process, I am finding that many people do not seem to have this clarity in their creative intent. For instance, we might know that we are God, yet we are not able to instantaneously create. It appears to be one thing to say that we are God, and another thing entirely to live it.

KIRAEL: This is the function of the veils you have agreed to come here with. It is a function of the ego that has been presented to you by your higher self so that you might do your journey to fully understand all the processes available in this Third Dimension. In this journey, we are all on various levels of enlightenment. Yes, masters and avatars can manifest instantaneously. But I assure you that as you grow in spirit, the time between the intent and the creation will become shorter and shorter. I have said many times that in your post-Shift fourth-dimensional reality, your thoughts will manifest instantaneously. In the meantime, it is in the highest of light that you continue on your path of enlightenment and that you simply do the journey. Take heart, my friend, all is in perfection.

Healing and the Four Pillars of Conscious Creation

How do the Four Pillars of Conscious Creation interweave with the process of healing?

KIRAEL: The Four Pillars of Conscious Creation are the actual weave of healing itself. When you decide to create a healing journey, you begin to realize where you came from and where you are going in this illusion. And that is what this whole illusion is about: your healing process. Whichever of the four bodies—the physical, emotional, mental, or spiritual—you might be working on, you soon find that the Four Pillars of Prayer, Meditation, Sleepstate Programming, and Masterminding interlace through the weave and fabric of the four bodies. And the total weave of the Four Pillars of Conscious Creation brings about the healing.

By praying and meditating, and by sleepstate progamming and masterminding in clarity on what you want to heal, you will experience healing that will first manifest in one of your four bodies. It will activate healing within the other bodies as well. In effect, healing within your emotional body will prompt healing in your physical body and so on. In essence, the healing presence of the Four Pillars weaves itself through the entire fabric of your beingness, to the point where you are healed on a myriad of levels.

What you discover then is *love*. Until that point, you have been caught up in the illusions of the human matrix and have lost sight of the warp and weave of love of which you are made. Now you are healing on new levels of consciousness. And although you may not see the strands of love interweaving through the healing process, you know and feel the beauty of what is taking place. You simply feel the light of healing and love within you. In the fullness of that light, you are cured. Is that simple enough?

When you are committed to making the Four Pillars of Conscious Creation a way of life, your life opens up to the fullness of the 90% consciousness, which is the 100% truth of who you truly are. You find that you are an endless flow of light, where there is no beginning, no end. There isn't even any weave or structure. There is only the light itself.

Lightworkers and the Four Pillars of Conscious Creation

If there are individuals that are using the Four Pillars with negative input, how do you counteract that? Can the Four Pillars be used to counteract negative energy forces?

KIRAEL: First of all, the Four Pillars can only be used in the negative force if your belief systems allow it to be negative. For instance, there are those that believe they can conjure up the force of a demon in their presence. And if those present can see the demon, then they, of course, can promote the demon. What happens is the force of the people present gives the demon life. It is their belief in the darkness that gives the darkness its life. Without such a belief system, the darkness could not exist other than as a conjured note of authority sparked by someone with a weakened mind. If a weakened mind is given a spark of authority, the darkened forces have no presence with which to behold itself, thus making it impossible to remain in this dimension. Those in another country sending dark energy your direction can only exist because you make allowances for their existence. If a spark of darkness is created in Southeast Asia, for example, and it is sent in this direction, it needs those in this country to grab hold of it to give it life; otherwise, it cannot exist.

As for Lightworkers, they need never fear darkness. They need never fear a dimmed society. For Lightworkers know they can control their immediate surroundings. And they know that joined together as a force of Lightworkers, they can control whatever they focus their light on.

The God Creator is Light. It creates everything. In order for you to turn something dark, it must have the force of your thoughts, the will of the word, to create it to be so. Therefore, that which is dark on your planet is *your* creation; and if it is your creation, you are responsible. If you are responsible, then you can change that for which you are responsible.

Closing Statement

In closing, I would suggest this to be your ultimate truth when you decide it to be: *You are in full control of this dimension.* There is nothing happening here without your permission. There is nothing happening here without your agreement. No matter what takes place, it is an agreement between you and the higher sources of Light.

When you learn to utilize the Four Pillars of Conscious Creation, you begin to design your outcomes to your own benefit, as opposed to accepting the outcomes and benefits of others. Once you are in control of your life, those that surround you will be in control of theirs as they align to your energy. Once you have a select energy force in control of the Four Pillars through Conscious Creation, you understand that you can take this level of awareness to its next level. And finally, you will draw the Shift nearer and you will be able to get through it in the greatest light possible.

Those choosing not to hear these words will still make it through the Shift, but they will have to stumble along the way. Those of you who choose to become Lightworkers and live by the Four Pillars of Conscious Creation will understand that life is your thought, trained by your will to act itself out through the word. You will find it to be that simple, my friends.

Good evening.

The Four Pillars discussed here are four of Kirael's Ten Principles of Conscious Creation: Truth, Trust, and Passion; Clarity, Communication, and Completion; and Prayer, Meditation, Sleepstate Programming, and Masterminding.

Also available: a ten-audiotape series by Kirael, "How to Have It All: The Ten Principles of Conscious Creation."

7 *Your Shifting Body:*
There is No Turning Back

Opening Statement

KIRAEL: Good evening.

In these times, there is a brand new understanding of the word *energy*. Energy is no longer something that is transferred between poles on a wire. Energy is something that is amplified by the human element, or the human embodiment process, and each portion of this energy must be sent out in such a fashion as to achieve the best results. You can no longer do the old-fashioned spirals that you have done in the past. The energy now needs to rise to a new level. Indeed, the Shift you have now entered is not a process that you are accustomed to. Why? Because this Shift has never before been experienced by human light.

Here to Experience the Shift

Each and every time the Creator's energy on the Earth plane has restructured its formation to another vibration, the Earth has first been evacuated of all human life. You have experienced catastrophes of great magnitude, such as the Ice Ages, as a way for the Creator to reset the Earth plane. Then, upon completion of the Earth's restructuring, the human light would evolve to the level where it could inhabit the Earth plane once more. And so it has been for eons of time.

At each stage of evolution, Mother Earth and her inhabitants would crawl slowly to the highest level of awareness. Humans would resume their journeys at the lowest evolutionary levels necessary to allow them to redo any lesson plans not completed in fullness. (This is how the Creator sees to it that nothing goes unlearned.) Then, when a point was reached that overtaxed the planet's system, the inhabitants would return to Light, followed by another great shift.

Listen carefully here: Each time a shift has taken place, the Earth has always evolved back to a level that allows every single energy pattern of existence on the planet the opportunity to resume old lesson plans as well as to move to new levels of evolution. Hence, your current Shift. This time, however, it will be different. In this Shift, a portion of the human experience will stay aboard planet Earth and ride the whole process through. In your current incarnation, it was established that if you, the human, could reach a certain level of awareness, you would then proceed through the Shift so that Creation could interact with this whole process through a six-sensory awareness. As I said at the beginning, this shall be the first time that Creation experiences the Shift through the human light.

Now, don't go running and screaming out the door. In this Shift, rather than an Ice Age that covers the Earth for literally thousands of years, there are only the "three days of darkness." I'd say that is a pretty good deal! [See *Kirael: The Great Shift*, Chapter 8, "Three Days of Darkness."]

Before you give a big sigh of relief and say, "Thank you, God," remember that *you* made a commitment to your Creator to remain on Earth through the Shift, and you will utilize your physical body to do so. For this reason, you are now learning about the rising vibration of the human body. It is also the reason why you have begun the process of shifting into the light body before we get to the three days of darkness.

Thank "God-ness," right? Yes, each of you is being aligned to this new energy. The photon energy around your Earth is vibrating at very rapid levels for this very reason. I might add that your galactic brothers and sisters are quite proud of the gains that you are making. You human beings can be extremely proud of what you are doing down here—especially those of you in the Lightworker corps who have committed yourselves to the healing arts.

What is the task of the Lightworkers at this stage of the Shift? Essentially, Lightworkers are experiencing rapid growth in their own evolution. They are raising their vibrational energy forces. For example, many are finding that the time for holding on to jobs that no longer serve their highest growth is past. They have moved on from jobs and careers that offer little more than job security. Job security never did exist, especially now. Hence, Lightworkers have the task of moving on to new levels of energy within the human journey.

Did you know that there are certain people living on the Earth plane today who can literally exist on prana breathing alone? They have learned how to raise their vibration beyond the need for food as sustenance. Well, is it not truth that if one can, all can? For no one has unique energies over here; no one is more special than the other. You are all Creator energies. Some have simply chosen to move to a new level.

Each chooses how to see that new level of energy. Those of you who enjoy eating big, fat juicy steaks might say people who live off prana are strange. Others might think people that only eat Creator-given energies such as fruits and vegetables have something wrong with them. Those who have a good steady diet of Creator food, which comes from the plant world might view people who eat animal flesh as being "less than." Well, you need to stop all that and let each person evolve at his or her own rate. Better yet, you, the Lightworkers, need to be concerned with making yourselves available to those who want to move forward.

You must always be willing to relinquish the levels in life that you have attained and be ready to move on to the next. Back in the time of Lemuria, my friends, the entire Lemurian society was based on a council format. Once you became a councilmember, the entire focus of your light was to replace yourself and move off the council. Moving off a council represented for you a new level of awareness and a new sense of freedom. It also meant new levels of learning and responsibilities as you joined another council.

Whilst serving on a council, each was to focus on the light of the council, the decision body, if you will. If you were the head of a council, your entire reality was to inspire as many people as you could and say, "Come, come, come! Let me show you what I am doing!" The minute one of them said, "I'm ready to take your place on the council," there was no negotiation; you moved on. Naturally, you were responsible to look in on the process for a period of time to be sure your replacement was capable of filling your job on the council. After that, you were relieved of the responsibility of being in charge and would move to the next level of evolution.

What I am saying is that from here forward, the Shift is all about motion. If you want to say that in a clever way, what is the one thing that you are all here to experience? It is emotion: evolutionary energy in motion. I would like you to see *e-motion* as *evolutionary motion* because that is really what the emotions of the Earth human are all about.

Questions & Answers

Mass Ascensions

It is fascinating to know that we are going to be the first humans to experience the Shift in a conscious, awakened state. At the time of previous shifts on the Earth plane, how did those populations go "home?"

KIRAEL: There have been a number of society releases, and each time, the people have not died but have literally awakened at a given moment. In this awakening, they have gone beyond the ego system to where they realized that they were Creator Light.

Such an awakening takes place at the cellular level: you immediately disengage the 10% thought systems and go into the 90%. In the 90%, or the All That Is, you are capable of "de-molecularizing" your system and you return into Light again.

Could you give us a sense of how long it takes on this dimension for this awakening to occur?

KIRAEL: Here on this dimension, you don't have anything to measure it by, but I would say an awakening would take place in less than seconds. Remember that time is an illusion and therefore doesn't have any value other than what you give it. For this reason, it is impossible to say "less than seconds" because the awakening takes place en masse. But imagine this: At precisely the same moment, everyone knows what is taking place, so there is a certain element of elation. And no, there is no time for fear. It is the same as me telling you how long it takes for you to transition at the point of your supposed death, when it is happening to you at that very moment.

There are archaeological remains of lost civilizations on the Earth plane, where the inhabitants seem to have disappeared, leaving behind signs that they instantaneously vanished from their dwellings. Is this what you are talking about—mass ascensions?

KIRAEL: Absolutely.

You have also said previously that there were populations that went underground during other shifts on the Earth plane. Was God the Creator willing for all that to happen just because the Creator is always interested in experiencing new things?

KIRAEL: They *are* the Creators. Eventually, you need to stop separating your energies from the Creator and Creation. I know that this is very difficult because you have been taught to hold God in high esteem. Doesn't the medium occasionally read from the Bible during Sunday church services? Well, the Bible acknowledges that God is Light. It doesn't say God is Light *something*; it just says God is Light. When you realize that you are the Creator and that you have chosen to enjoy your Creator's Light in this type of a vibration through "particle-ization," only then can you experience what the Creator might experience in the truest form.

Is there is a lot of religion-based fear surrounding "the rapture" because of mass ascensions that have already taken place? Is that why people think it is going to happen again this time?

KIRAEL: That is precisely where fear will come from, because it is in the cellular consciousness. Each one of you knows of this exactly. [*"Wow"* is heard throughout the audience.]

I get a kick out of you going "Wow." Did you know that "wow" indicates the awakening stages of your cellular conscious? It is when the 10% brain becomes over-evolved and you don't have words to put with it. "Wow" is nothing more than you overcompensating for your 10% limitations.

Your Shifting Weight

I have so many questions on the human light never having experienced a shift before, and about the human embodiment going through a lot of changes as it ascends into its light body. But first, how is the physical embodiment reacting to the photon energy, the Sun's polar shift, and to the amplification of the magnetic grid?

KIRAEL: To begin, it is important to understand that we have already entered into the Shifting process. With the different magnetic poles and the different pulls of the Sun affecting the polar energies, many seem to be experiencing an awful lot of aches and pains in their physical body these days. All of a sudden, many people are becoming conscious of losing weight, even though their weight hasn't changed much. Others are feeling they have gained a little bit more than they think they should. This might not make sense, but if you are beginning to feel heavy, it is because your own cellular awareness is automatically telling you to eat up a storm to get heavier. In other words, you have to be particularly watchful of the physical body right now.

Know that all of this is due to energy shifts that are focused on the Earth plane right now. The pains that seem to be descending upon you are actually the body's attempts to shift from its density into the light energy. It is experiencing an abrupt increase of energetic thought patterns taking place within the cellular consciousness. When this happens, the tendency is to over-react because you don't know what is going on. Your 10% brain is simply attempting to assimilate the information it is receiving, and what it is receiving is that you feel heavier.

The truth is, you are getting lighter, but you feel heavier. So, the first thing your 10% brain does is focus on what you are eating. The best way to deal with this is to refocus the information in your 10% brain and disseminate it back to the cellular consciousness. You will find yourself eating less as you shift into the light body energy.

However, you will also find your body storing up energy because it feels it has gone into a starvation mode. Your 10% brain, mostly recognizing fear, feels you are gearing up for famine. When that happens, the physical body will begin to store fat energy in response to your 10% thought systems. In short, the defense mechanism of the 10% thought system, based on your fear-driven society issues, will cause you to actually gain weight. You will become heavier in an attempt to stay closer to the Earth plane.

The same applies to any diet that you try. First, the body thinks that you are trying to prepare for a famine. So, it takes everything it has and puffs it up into what we call fat energy, or what I would call "salvageable reinforcements." But the minute you come off the diet and eat, the fat energy just dumps on top of everything and poof—up goes your weight! The reason that diets don't really work is because the psychological part of the body, or the cellular consciousness, is acting as it has for thousands of years. For thousands of years, you would eat, then you wouldn't eat; you had famine, and then you would have great times. All this is recorded deep in your cellular consciousness.

When you become aware that your cellular consciousness well out-thinks your 10% thought systems, you will realize why you are always lagging behind what your physical body wants to do. Your physical presence is making up its mind long before the 10% brain can calculate the information that is coming to it. So, by the time your 10% realizes that you are getting a bit chubby, the physical body is well into its storage mode, and you immediately run to the doctor or buy a new diet book. Or worse, you starve yourself.

Starving yourself is the worst thing you can do. The minute you do that, the body's cellular consciousness goes, "Uh-oh, another famine" because the physical body is suddenly not receiving the proteins, minerals, and other nutrients it normally gets. The body then proceeds to double its efforts to store every single, minute particle it can find by converting it into fat—the same as when you are on a diet. You wind up all bubbled out. Your body is now in crisis modality. So, what do you do next? Normally, you get all huffed and say, "To heck with it! I am going to eat anything I want!" Then everybody is happy—except you. You get bigger and bigger, until you decide that it scares you, and you try dieting all over again.

My friends, you can only diet through prayer, meditation and sleepstate programming. That is the one diet available that truly works.

Does that mean we can retain our normal body weight with our regular eating habits? In other words, we shouldn't panic?

KIRAEL: It is the panic that is really costly. Understand that the panic comes from the 10% thinking, for it lags far behind the cellular body process.

Do you understand that the entirety of your 10% awareness is the learned understanding of the current dimension? Very little of your past life issues are found within the 10% brain. Instead, they are laced throughout your cellular consciousness. Only when it comes time to work on a given past life issue does it move into the 10% awareness.

You take the 10% awareness that is based in fear, and you make decisions based on that. In your 10% thinking you don't lose weight because you love yourself; you lose weight because you are afraid of becoming obese or because you think you are not pretty. That is why you lose weight. On top of that, it is almost guaranteed that losing weight also involves the fear of not keeping the weight off. If that is your fear, don't bother.

My friends, what if you only want to lose weight because you love yourself enough to understand and align with your cellular consciousness? It is time to realize that the Shift is affecting all of you on cellular levels. Your cellular consciousness is taking a predominant role within each of you, affecting everything that is manifesting in your life.

With fear-based 10% thought systems escalating, you will also find yourself trying to compensate for shifts in energy. This will only cause another escalation of over-reaction in the 10%. You will also recognize that the Four Pillars of Conscious Creation—prayer, meditation, masterminding and sleepstate programming—which I have been teaching for so many years on this Earth plane, are the tools needed to resonate to the changes in your physical body and to find alignment with your cellular consciousness.

For those who are still searching for heaven in the sky, I would suggest you search within to find it. When you realize that heaven only exists within you, you find the blessed light of who you are and the fact that you are Creation. You begin to see that what matters most is making changes within yourself, rather than trying to change the outside world to match up with your belief systems. You understand that you no longer need to change the fears that fuel your fear-driven society.

At the same time, Lightworkers cannot take the attitude, "I am a Lightworker; therefore, I don't want to deal with those who are fear-based anymore." You most assuredly do. You most definitely need to be a Lightworker, because there are not enough of you yet to sustain Earth and her inhabitants post-Shift. I would say you will need at least two billion to really sustain Earth's energy.

Your Shifting Body, Liquid Diets and Fasts

I recently tried a 10-day liquid diet where I drank only a concoction of water, lemon juice and molasses. As soon as I got off the diet, the weight came back, in part, due to a new-found pleasure in eating. Now I find myself fighting to keep the weight down, which I now understand comes from fear. So how do I handle this struggle between the cellular consciousness and the 10% mind?

KIRAEL: There is only one way out: prayer. I would suggest that you sit down with my medium and pray. He prays with great passion over his food before eating. You might direct a prayer to your higher self and all the energy forces that you are made up of, saying, "Please allow me to eat or ingest only what my body needs." In that way, I guarantee you will not finish everything on your plate, because you probably have more on your plate than your body needs. The average stomach is the size of your fist. So if you want to fill the stomach, that is how much you have to eat. Why not try to fill it to capacity, not to over-capacity?

Why not also raise the vibration of the food by praying over it? Now if there was a big slab of dead beef on your plate, you would have to say a pretty darn good prayer to raise its energy. It would be simpler with a beautiful salad on your plate, for that is the energy source that your Creator intended for you. Yes, I know it is difficult for you in the human world to remember that the Creator created the greens on your plate as your source of energy. Still, this is truth.

As for the liquid diet you were on, that was a form of starvation. You also punished your system by drinking some stuff that you didn't like the taste of, on top of depriving it of food. What did your fear-based mind say then? "We don't want this to happen again, so let's store up more in there to make sure she never does it again!"

So you don't recommend fasting?

KIRAEL: If you want to fast as a way of cleansing and if you pray your way through it, you are all right. It is best to pray into the fast, pray through the fast, and pray out of the fast so that your cellular consciousness is aware that you are not trying to starve it, but only to cleanse it. If you are sending this intent throughout your system while doing the cleansing, then your fast is somewhat accepted. But I don't suggest it as a rule.

Therefore, if you eat decently and eat small portions, you don't need to fast. Is that right?

KIRAEL: That is right, as long as you don't clog yourself up with fatty-type foods that are difficult to digest. If you remember that prayer can raise the vibration of the food you eat, then you can offset the tremendous demands placed on your physical body by foods not easily digested. You will soon find that the foods you choose to eat will either hinder or foster your light body transformation.

The cellular consciousness holds everything; it is the All That Is. So does it hold fears as well as the knowingness of Light?

KIRAEL: Yes, it handles whatever your 10% feeds down into it, thinking that is what you need to do in order to compensate for coming here.

Your Light Body

What is your definition of a light body?

KIRAEL: One of the definitions of a light body is the *capability of de-molecularization through the process of thought intent.* When you evolve into a light body, you have a higher molecular vibration. At a higher molecular vibration, you tap into the core of light. In fact, the cellular make-up of the human body is a mutual observance of both light particles and sound vibration. Your body holds the appearance of being solid; however, the light particles are constantly evolving from its core light.

When you enter the Earth plane, you begin life within a trinity of energies, each made up of light particles for the purpose of creating life on the material plane. First, there is the female egg; then comes the male sperm; and finally, the particle light of the God Creator, which holds the vibrational essence of your life plans. This trinity formation becomes known as *the signature cell*.

In the nine months in the mother's womb, the trinity of energies concentrate on appearing solid, using illusionary modification for the physical body to take shape. Once formed, the body remains in this vibration in order for the human to carry out the life plan, fully or partially, depending on the choices of the individual. Ultimately, it reunites with the fullness of the Creator's Light—still referred to as *death*.

Because of the Shift, many will find their physical bodies beginning to in-lighten, allowing the density of the body to dissipate. This is already taking place amongst those who regularly do prana breathing and engage in prayer and meditation and other spiritual practices. The more one enlightens the consciousness, the more in-lightened the body becomes as the light particles within each cell emanate energy from their core light. Hence, a light body.

As you become more light-bodied, some organs in your body will diminish to make room for others to grow in size. Take, for example, your lungs. The lungs of a human male extend about 7 inches at present, but in the new light body, the lungs will be reduced to approximately 2 1/2 inches. This will occur because the body will no longer need to consume as much oxygen as it does now. (Your lung capacity is automatically diminishing as you begin to breathe in *prana* throughout your body process.)

In turn, the thymus gland will have more room to expand. When restored to its original size, its function will be to interact more with other body parts in the cleansing process, or what we call "keeping the misaligned cellular knowledge out of the mirror visuals." This will help you to heal at a much more rapid pace.

Does the light body include an increasing number of DNA strands?

KIRAEL: Yes, you currently are at two and two, meaning two solid DNA strands and two vibrating DNA strands. But when you evolve to light body, they become four and four, which puts you into the fullness of light body at eight strands. There is first a period of transition, where you have four solid strands and two vibrating strands of DNA.

Your Expanding Chakra System

Will the functions of the three lower chakras be reduced during the Shift?

KIRAEL: For the most part, yes. However, I cannot say as an absolute that the three lower chakras will no longer exist after the Shift, for they will be needed in certain cases. Let me explain.

Following the three days of darkness that transition you out of the current matrix energy, there are those who will come through at Level 1 and Level 2. Those at Level 1 and 2 after the Shift will maintain a human fragmentation rather than go into a hologram or be dispersed into Light. Those at Level 1— and listen carefully to what I am saying—will need to believe without a doubt that they have the three base chakras in order to complete all the unfinished lesson plans they have accumulated over the many centuries of coming to the Earth plane. Level 1 literally allows you to complete those lesson plans.

If you attain mid-Level 3 and up, you will not have use for them. I absolutely guarantee that they will not exist. [For more on the Seven Levels of Awareness in the Fourth Dimension, see *Kirael Volume II: The Genesis Matrix*, Chapter 7.]

What physical symptoms might women experience in the process of the lower three chakras diminishing?

KIRAEL: You won't like the answer to this one: Most of the women will begin to add on physical weight—not a great deal, hopefully, for your sakes. You might also find your sexual drive diminishing for a short period of time, but when it comes back, your husbands will be very happy. Your appetites will shift because many of the changes will begin in your lower chakras. You will even walk differently. All this is a result of your body refocusing itself to the higher Light energy. It is a bit disheveling in the beginning stages, but I assure you that it all does come into alignment.

I think that a lot of people will experience fear when they hear that the three base chakras are shutting down. I too have difficulty with that because I want to ascend into my highest light body. At the same time, I am still very human and want to stay that way. So how can I alleviate that fear?

KIRAEL: When I say to the physical world that you are going to lose your bottom chakras, most of you will say, "Oh, my God, but I've had them forever!" [*laughter*] What is that? It is fear. And whenever you do something from fear, you compensate for it in the cellular consciousness. In most cases, you put on weight, thinking that more weight will somehow magically hold you to the Earth plane.

How about not saying that the three lower chakras are going to be dissolved, eradicated, or diminished? How about simply recognizing that when you no longer have use for them, you will release them to your own love and light? In that sense, you are not really losing anything.

Will the fourth chakra, the heart chakra, become the base chakra?

KIRAEL: Yes, because in the light body there is no need for the grounding from the red, orange and yellow chakras. Those three lower chakras have been necessary for the very solid third-dimensional thinkers who need a very physical world to operate in. They have been necessary to maintain the physical body and for the unfolding of your lesson plans.

As you move into your light body, you move into a higher vibration of understanding, where you center yourself at the very heart core. For this reason, the fourth chakra is now becoming the base of your light body.

Can the base chakra evolve beyond the fourth? I have got a feeling that my base chakra is at the crown. How far in the Fourth Light does the light body evolve?

KIRAEL: To attain the highest level in the Fourth Light, or the Fourth Dimension, you will need to understand love in its purest form. Most people will acknowledge the green, or heart chakra as the new base chakra. When you come from heart, you are in a space of unconditional love, right? But when you look at the rest of the chakras, they will begin a blending formation, making it difficult to consider a base chakra at that time.

A moment ago you said that you thought the crown chakra could be your base. It likely could be. However, from Guidance we would suggest to you that through the major parts of the Shift, most would recognize the green chakra as the base chakra. After the Shift, those of you that have evolved past that measure will be able to choose your base chakra because it will be on a fluctuating scale at that point.

As we increase our DNA strands, are we adding on new chakra points?

KIRAEL: The chakra points are already there, but at this point, your body cannot phase into their light very easily because of the density of your body. If you listen carefully to my medium when he speaks on healing, you will understand that the density of the Third Dimension, or the dramatic space of your total illusion, is your 10% mind telling you that you have a physical life.

As that thinking diminishes, you allow the higher self to play a more active role in your evolutionary processes. This is where it gets tricky. It is often impossible for you within your present body system to see when you are operating in the light body space; that is, when you are working with the higher self. Being so trapped in the linear, third-dimensional spacing, you believe that this dimension has reality. For this reason, you have needed the red, orange and yellow chakras for the grounding they provide.

Once the need for the lower three chakras is released, you enter into the light system. In that space, you have conscious awareness of your light body. Your biggest challenge will be returning to deal with third-dimensional matters, even though you have greater light body awareness.

For those of you who will no longer wish to deal with the third-dimensional density post-Shift, there is another solution. You will be able to send another fragment of your higher energy into the body system. More specifically, your higher self will aspect itself for the third time, forming a trinity with you and the higher self. And together, you will join forces to do long-distance work.

How many new chakras are there going to be beyond the current seven?

KIRAEL: Four. They are the connectors of the light body that allow your light body to function in the physical world.

What colors are the eighth, ninth, tenth and eleventh chakras? And what about the twelfth and thirteenth chakras?

KIRAEL: Wait! Stop! Why don't you just concentrate on the ones that will get you to the Fifth Light? [*laughter*] Actually, one chakra will be pink, and another, a very, very beautiful blue-green. You will also have a chakra of an ivory color and another more golden in color. Now, if you were to take those four and bring them into one light, the new color would be beyond your imagination. The blending of the colors of the new chakras in the right hues is the fullness of all chakras, including the ones that are diminishing at this time. In full vibration, they appear as one color. So, my friend, the colors of the thirteenth, fourteenth, fifteenth, nineteenth—even the forty-third chakra—are not important at this time.

Do the new chakra colors combined make a pale yellow color?

KIRAEL: It probably resonates closer to gold, but you wouldn't be far off the mark.

While working on a person's hip in a healing today, I saw the colors blue and purple coming through. Both of us also saw a lemon-gold-blue-green color. Is that part of the chakra color system that you are talking about?

KIRAEL: Absolutely. What happened was that you probably created a "cellular amassation," which can only be taken apart by color itself once it coagulates in a particular space. Although sound is oftentimes the answer, in this particular case, it has to come apart by light. Your higher self is probably sending this new information to you. This will allow other people to see it so that, together, you can discuss it and develop new healing techniques.

Chakras and Healing

In thinking about the lower three chakras and the issues often related to them, is there something new that we can incorporate into our healing work?

KIRAEL: Yes, check with your higher self on what you need to incorporate into your healing work. In your case, you have got a really super higher self that is going to tell you everything anyway.

The key here is that the lower three chakras are beginning to release their energy force, which understandably makes most people try that much harder to hold on to them. Let's take the very bottom chakra, the red one, as an example. As it begins to compress, the red chakra fears death, much like anything else in your world. It feels a form of death and reacts by tightening up in a defensive modality.

You in the healing world are probably thinking, "Well, if they are phasing out, I don't need to work on them anymore." No, you probably need to work on them more than ever at that point. As a healer, you need to know what is taking place. It is not so much about telling people what is happening to them, but more about helping their chakras relax.

Do the lower chakras remain open or do they close down fully in this stage of shifting to the light body?

KIRAEL: Good question. They remain open to some extent, as is needed for evolutionary processing. Meaning, you will now find many *diseases* dropping down to the lower chakras. These chakras serve to store your yet-to-be completed lesson plans as you align to your light body. The problem is that in the interim many of those lesson plans may become solid enough to manifest as lower abdominal diseases, especially in the urinary tract, the sexual organs, and so on. The lesson plans can become so compressed at that point that you will feel compelled to bring them to completion, and your healers will recognize them as such.

Now understand this: the medium is going to teach you more about this when you are ready. But first, he needs more than a handful of you to be ready as healers. For instance, you now have what we call "tag-line diseases," which are diseases within which you can follow the interruption of a physical third-dimensional thought. You can actually follow the line of thought from where it interrupts the third-dimensional vibration to the actual segment of awareness. When you identify the precise point of interruption, you discover the process for healing the outer, physical body whilst simultaneously healing it within.

When I am doing healing work on someone who is acquiring light value and assessing their chakras with a pendulum, will I see those lower three chakras moving in an up-and-down motion?

KIRAEL: Yes. There is energetic movement through that chakra, and it is moving in a spiritual motion. It is moving in the Creator's Light, or infinity Light. This is always seen in the shape of a lazy-eight, or what you might recognize as the infinity sign. You will see the energy in the lower chakras literally moving up into the higher chakras, then coming back down in a cleansing motion. Again, you don't lose the chakras; hence, there is no need for fear.

The chakras are literally evolving; the entire body is evolving, for you are all a product of evolutionary light. Remember, each of you on the Earth plane has chosen to come here as evolutionary light. It has always been a choice of your evolution, but now it is a greater choice. You, as part of Creation, have chosen to make this great attempt to utilize a physical presence through a Shift process as never done before.

Other Physical Shifts in the Body

What other changes of the human body can we look forward to post-Shift?

KIRAEL: When you enter the Fourth Dimension post-Shift, your brain will be able to calculate 27 times faster than it currently does. You will not have to wear glasses because you will be able to hear what you are seeing.

In the Fourth Dimension, transporting yourself from one place to another will require a process of "de-molecularization." For the most part, you will use a *multitude reactor* device. For instance, if you wished to move your energy from Hawaii to somewhere in Ohio, you would need this device that would activate a multitude of energies to react to one space. Actually, only those at Level 3 and below will need a multitude reactor device to move from one place to the other. Those at Level 4 and higher will be able to de-molecularize at will.

I have been experiencing tremendous changes in the lower part of my neck which feel at times like a cracking open and shifting of my hindbrain. And it seems that most of the healings I am receiving are centered in this area. Can you elaborate on how this ties into the Shift?

KIRAEL: You are a doctor [addressing the speaker], so you know that that area is also where the major stem of the nervous system is located, right? Your light body must first be erected through the nervous system and that is why you are feeling changes there. The good thing is that you will receive a lot of help from Guidance on resetting the nervous system. Guidance will begin to exchange information systems with you through the left and right sections of your brain. They will mesh the information and download it into your nervous system, which will then create the light body system of the human body. Guidance will often work with you in your sleep and at other times when you are awake.

I would say that sixty to ninety days from the time you first began to notice the physical sensations, you will also feel as though you are losing weight. When you step on the scales, your weight loss will be confirmed. However, you won't see it visibly in the physical world because you are becoming an en-lightened embodiment. That is one of the beauties of the Shift. You are just a little ahead of most people.

Your Kundalini Energy

As the base chakra moves up into the higher chakra areas, what is happening to the kundalini, which is the energy of consciousness originating at the base of the spine? Is it the same type of energy flow?

KIRAEL: The *kundalini* will take on a higher vibration. As the *kundalini* energy rises, it will become denser and more definable by those who work and practice with its energy force. This is unusual because normally when something takes on a higher vibration, it loses the original definition of the energy.

Will the kundalini be more definable in that we will see its energy movement more clearly?

KIRAEL: Yes, and you will have a clearer sense of how to work with it. The *kundalini* will be self-defined, refocused. I can't go into this in great depth at this time. For now, let's just say that the *kundalini* will play a great part in the reduction of egotism.

I understand you to say that as the kundalini becomes more self-defined, it will become a beacon of light. To achieve that, you will need to experience a healing process that moves you into that knowingness. Then from there you can direct that energy with intent. Can you comment on that?

KIRAEL: *Kundalini* energy can be part of the healing process. However, healing is still often misconstrued as trying to heal only the physical body. Hopefully, by now, you know the physical body is the body you need to worry about the least. The healing of your physical body will always follow whatever you are healing in your emotional, mental, or spiritual bodies. In addition, I would say that a large percentage of you are working with past life issues in this lifetime that you brought along to heal with the greatest of intent in your cellular consciousness.

Is this why there is a predominance in the healing arts dealing specifically with past life issues?

KIRAEL: It should be. There are a lot of people who don't believe in past lives, and that is a large part of why they need to heal. Are you to convince them of this? No, you are to work with them in the highest light that you can muster.

Have you noticed that people often initially resist thinking about past life possibilities, but after a few healing sessions they begin to ask questions? Why is this? Well, when my medium is working on healing processes with them, he is always *inner-lighting* them. In so doing, he helps to bring their light to a higher level so that they can remember to heal.

Everybody is Creator Light. Everybody has the same love; some just choose more density to live in than others. All begin life in the womb. All are born, and like Adam and Eve, they take on an ego system that aids them in a "forgetting process." This opens the way to healing karma and to working on lesson plans brought into this lifetime. Then as you heal your past life issues, your cellular consciousness is cleansed and your core light is strengthened.

Your Own DNA

I recently found some galactic DNA healing techniques that I am interested in working with. I sense that I am being guided to incorporate them in my healing work.

KIRAEL: Maybe you will, eventually. But right now, the galactics want you to incorporate them first into your own DNA. As a rule, you can learn about DNA from a book, but you can't learn the inner workings of it from a book. You must first work with your own DNA. For that, you have to work from within.

Okay, so how do I do that?

KIRAEL: Oh, I would suggest I pick you up about 3:00 a.m. tonight and take you out to the Pleiades. We will visit one of their systems so I can show you what I am talking about. That is the best I can do for you.

That sounds wonderful.

KIRAEL: I am not kidding! Anybody who wants to join us can meet me above her house about 3:00 a.m. I will take people anytime they want to go; they just need to tell me when and where they would like to go.

And with that, I will be taking my leave.

Good evening.

8 THE OTHER ASPECTS OF YOU: SPLINTERS, WALK-INS AND TWIN FLAMES

Opening Statement

KIRAEL: Good evening.

What we shall bring forth this evening may be a bit of a stretch for the average mind in the Third Dimension. I mean that only as a positive, for what I share with you is that on this Earth dimension *you are simply a physical manifestation of your totality.* Once you open to this truth, you no longer need to wrestle with the unseen spirit part of you; you need only to allow your physical self to flow with it. Once you accept this as truth, much of what I say this night can be seen in a different light.

Splinters

Let's begin with the higher self, or your *essential self,* as I often refer to it. The higher self is the part of you in constant awareness of all reality focuses, while maintaining a connection with you at all times. It is ever ready to be of service to you, wanting nothing more than for you to understand why you have committed to this evolutionary journey. Hence, if the higher self finds in your life journey a blockage or resistance to its evolution, it may decide to add another portion of itself by means of a splinter of energy.

What is a *splinter?* It is a vibrational segment of the higher self that enters into the vibratory system of your human light body. It is a higher vibrating segment powerful enough to change the focus of your energy and move your life in a more desired direction. The challenge to humans is to release any fears of change, and in so doing, the new splinter can transition into your energy system smoothly. So I would say to you, welcome splinters into your life, for they are a sure sign of growth. More importantly, know that splinters are added only at the measure your higher self knows you can handle.

How do you know when a new splinter is coming in? Usually when you are experiencing some moderate changes in your life, you can be sure that your higher self is being very gentle with you. It is checking to see whether you are on the path that you truly desire. If, on the other hand, you begin to re-evaluate your old belief systems and sense a powerful shift within your own energy forces, then your higher self has determined that you need to be "jump-started" a bit. It means that you are ready to move at a more rapid pace, and your higher self utilizes the splinter energy to bring you into greater alignment with your life plan.

In some cases, a new splinter may enter of which you remain completely unaware. At other times, you may receive a succession of splinters into your current reality. In any case, simply know that your higher self is guiding you to open to new levels of awareness. And let me forewarn you: if you suspect you are losing your mind and nothing around you makes sense, relax. It may just be your higher self's way of bringing an entirely new part of your total self on board.

Once you have discovered that completing one journey simply leads to new, more fulfilling experiences, your higher self becomes extremely elated with you. It begins to close out your journeys at a more rapid rate, offering you even higher challenges of experience. At this point, however, many of you will start saying, "Boo-hoo, boo-hoo. My life has run amuck. I can't keep track of all of the things I am going through right now." Perhaps you can—if you would make an ally of your higher self using the Four Pillars of Conscious Creation as your guide.

With that said, shall we open up to questions?

Questions & Answers

Aspects Usually Come in Threes

How many aspects of self does the higher self put on the Earth plane at the same time?

KIRAEL: The higher self will usually "aspect" itself into a trinity created of three aspects, although there is no guarantee of having any other aspects on the Earth plane at any given time. Spiritual seekers normally have at least two of their potential aspects on the Earth plane. However, when the higher self sees that a planet is about to undergo a new kind of shifting process, the higher self wants to garner as much knowledge of the experience that it possibly can. Hence, it arranges that all three of its aspects be on the planet at the same time.

At a certain point the higher self can decide to bring two aspects "home" to the Creator's Light and leave one on Earth, or it can decide to have all three on entirely different planetary systems. But most often, the higher self will focus three aspects of itself onto a single plane simultaneously, forming a trinity light formation from which to learn.

A Challenge: Only One Aspect on Earth

Is it rigorous if you are the only aspect of your higher self on the Earth?

KIRAEL: Oh, yes, it is, my friend. It is rigorous. When your higher self has more than one aspect on this dimension, it has time to entrust itself with all of them. But when you come as the sole aspect of your higher self, it is so focused on you that it just can't wait to help you. In other words, it just can't wait to push you forward. The truth is that you are in for a real rock-and-roll ride if you are the only aspect of a higher self on this dimension.

Would the emotional body be the most challenged if there were only one aspect here on Earth?

KIRAEL: Well, that is probably a loaded question because when you are in a sun-star system such as planet Earth, your emotions are one of your main focuses. It is your emotions that your higher self utilizes to guide you through the different processes that you experience.

Yes, when your emotions rise and fall in extremes, you can be sure that your higher self has designed you to move at a very rapid pace in this lifetime. And for this reason, you will move through your emotions very rapidly, sometimes finding yourself extra-creative. "Extra-creative"—I got myself out of that one, didn't I?

Does "extra-creative" mean that you cry a lot?

KIRAEL: Don't go there. I just got myself out of that and you are not getting me back in! [*laughter*]

God is Not Separate from the Process

If 10% thinking is being human and 100% knowing is God, what would the percentage of the higher self be? Does that make sense?

KIRAEL: Not really, because you are defining the Creator and then separating It, which cannot be separated. You are the Creator, my friend, pretending to vibrate at a 10% reality focus of a brain divided into two parts. The whole of the brain is Creator Light. The whole of the system is the Creator. The entirety of the Creator is the existence of the spiritual journey or whatever journey you have chosen. Therefore, you cannot define what is not separated.

Sources of Splinters

You have spoken about the higher self sending splinters of energy to its human part in order to move that human part to a new experience of its journey. Are there other sources from which the higher self can gather energy for that splinter or does it always come from the higher self?

KIRAEL: It is a grand question, and I will use the likes of a computer to explain that to you. If you understand how a floppy disk is utilized in a computer, you can see how a splinter works like a floppy disk. If your higher self sees that there is something to learn from your brethren in the Pleiades, it will receive this information from them on a type of floppy disk. The information from the floppy disk is then merged with your higher self and downloaded into you through a splinter. So the answer is an emphatic yes. You can receive splinters from other formats of life that will integrate with your system of thought.

Your Higher Self Has a Plan

I have received splinters vibrating at such high levels that it has been difficult to raise my vibration high enough to actively work with them. Then it seems that they leave, and splinters of lower vibrations remain that are easier to work with. Is it possible for us to request from our higher selves a splinter at a specific vibration as opposed to just receiving one?

KIRAEL: Very seldom do I suggest the answer of "no" in any of our conversations, but I do in this case. I don't mean to diminish you as a human, but your human part which is controlled by the 10% mind has little, if any, idea of the full quest. Until you are a one-brained unit, meaning until your human two-lobed brain merges and becomes one, you have no idea of the quest that you are truly on. Hence, it is the higher self choosing to move you along at a more rapid rate that enables you to receive these splinters. Believe me, this decision is never made by you at this level of awareness.

When your higher self downloads a splinter into you that vibrates so high that your life seems unbearable, the only way to lock it in is through the Four Pillars of Conscious Creation. By raising your vibration through prayer and meditation, and by setting your intentions clearly in your sleepstate programming and masterminding, you can bring yourself to resonate at the higher vibration. Otherwise, the new splinter will not adjust itself smoothly to match your vibration. The new splinter does not want to be what and who you are; it wants to move you to the next level. That is why it has come. Hence, you must strive to raise yourself to the higher vibration.

To be quite candid about it, should you try to tell the higher self, "Might you give me just a wee smaller one next time?" it won't listen to a word that you are saying. This is because it is the plan and you are the plan, and the plan together you are.

New Splinters and Colds

I used to get colds two or three times a year and friends would often say, "Oh, you are getting a new splinter." Could you comment on the correlation between the two?

KIRAEL: It is actually a simple answer. Colds are the consequences of a system that needs to slow down and relax. So when the higher self is attempting to move you at a more rapid rate by bringing in a splinter of higher energy, the body will often over-generate its energy, which manifests as symptoms of a cold. A cold is the body's way of settling you down so it can do its work. It gives you time to lie down and sleep, to adjust and see things in a new perspective while the new splinter settles itself within your vibratory system. The cold is a respite period. So yes, oftentimes, there is a correlation between a splinter and catching what you call a cold.

New Splinters and Your Emotions

You have said that new splinters may come through of which we are completely unaware. Is it also possible that splinters will come through and impact primarily the emotional body rather than the physical body?

KIRAEL: I wouldn't say it is a possibility; I would say it is almost a guarantee. If you really want to detect a splinter, you will detect it much sooner in the emotional body than in any other of your four bodies. Now where the emotional body is normally the first to react to a new splinter, the mental body is usually the last to pick it up. The spiritual body, on the other hand, is actually looking forward to the boost of energy from the new splinter.

Your emotional body becomes frustrated because it now must anticipate making new adjustments after having just come into alignment with the previous splinter. So when the emotions sense that a new splinter is coming, it automatically reacts to it. But let me also say that you wouldn't be getting a splinter if the higher self didn't feel that you had already become complacent with your current level of awareness.

Your Higher Self Likes Baptisms

When Master Jesus was baptized, he became the Christ Light and brought this beautiful Light onto the Earth plane. So when we—spirits pretending to be human—decide to be baptized in the Light of Creation, do we bring in a splinter?

KIRAEL: Oftentimes, when a new splinter of energy is not aligning as planned, the higher self will move to baptism for the beautiful blessings baptism offers. Hence, when you decide to go through a baptismal process, it is often because you have received a splinter and are aligning the rest of your energy to it.

When you are baptized, you are saying to the self that you have claimed your ability to understand that you are Light, and that you are now willing to rise into that Light in a dramatic way. Through baptism in the name of Jesus, you are moved to accept your Light in the Light of Christ and you honor the process of conscious creation with the Creator Energy Force. Baptism is your declaration that you are ready to evolve yourself into the Light through the Christ Consciousness within you.

On another level, baptism is basically a jolt of energy. It is an amplification of the Light that moves you to new levels, thereby making way for you and the new splinter of energy to come into better alignment.

Splinters and Oversouls

Is it possible for a higher self to send a splinter to another higher self within the same soul family?

KIRAEL: The soul family is only allowed to define itself through the proper channels designed by the God Creator. Each higher self is already an aspect of a soul family. Thus, it cannot extend another splinter of energy into a related aspect. To offshoot into another aspect would make no sense; the soul family would be collecting the same information from the energy forces of two higher selves at the same time.

Can the higher self go further up into the oversoul for splintered energy?

KIRAEL: I assure you that the higher self will do almost anything to *avoid* returning to the oversoul. If you return to the oversoul, it means you are back there for correction. If that is the case, it is very likely that you will receive a download of information that will take the entirety of your system out of the flow. The oversoul is nothing more than the housing of all knowledge. [For more information on Oversouls and Soul Families, see *Kirael Volume II: The Genesis Matrix*, Chapter 6.]

Twin Flames are Connected at Core Essence

What is the meaning of "twin flames"?

KIRAEL: Twin flames would be much like having twins here on the Earth plane. It is when you have an exact, replicated source from a defined single energy core, with the emphasis on the word *core*. Twin flames occur when a defined energy core breaks itself into two pieces and both pieces decide to move out into the same atmospheric condition at the same level of consciousness.

Twin flames are exact replicas of each other because there is no defined ability to process separation within their core essence. They are separated by thought alone. Hence, they are always placed at great distances from each other because the higher self knows that if the two should fill the same space, there would be no process of separation.

Nevertheless, you will often find younger souls searching out their twin flames, not knowing that by meeting, they chance blowing up half of the face of your planet. Two cosmic energies as powerful as the force of twin flames cannot entertain the same space. Should this occur, there would be an explosion of light that is insurmountable. It would outweigh any of your tools of destruction such as bombs.

Twin Flames at the Shift

At the time of the Shift, what happens to twin flames?

KIRAEL: One of the twin flames is absorbed back into the higher self and the other stays embodied; one goes home and one stays aboard the planet.

What determines which one stays and which one goes?

KIRAEL: With twin flames, the higher self would make the determination as to which of itself would remain in a body and which would return home. Believe me; the one coming home is more highly celebrated than the one left behind.

A Walk-In is Not a Splinter

How would you describe a "walk-in"?

KIRAEL: A walk-in, my friend, takes place when one lifetime journey has been fully completed, while a useful body presence still remains. (That is, if you haven't ruined your body from cigarettes, alcohol or stress.) In other words, a walk-in process can take place when you have kept yourself in a strong physical presence, your entire lesson plan is complete, and your higher self has decided that its aspect in that particular body essence is no longer of value to its growth. At that point, your higher self will allow another aspect of the same soul family to explore this level of reality by occupying the body that remains.

Two possibilities exist when all lesson plans are completed in fullness in a given journey. The simplest possibility is the agreement made when the higher self chooses to replace one aspect of itself with another aspect of itself, using the same physical body. (This would not be a splinter of energy, but an aspect with an entirely different blueprint.) When all is set, arrangements are made to release the vibration of the old aspect so the new aspect can be entered in. This is one form of a walk-in.

Now let us look at the other possibility. Suppose that the higher self is quite satisfied with all of its aspects on Earth. It is very happy with the way all of its aspects are operating in all generated forces. Yet one aspect with a decently functioning physical body no longer has the will to be here after having completed all its lesson plans. So the higher self returns into what is called the oversoul, where it selects an aspect of another higher self to make the exchange. This is another form of a walk-in that happens quite often in the Earth matrix.

How does this take place? I will give you the short explanation in hopes that you may be clear with it. Let's say you are the energy within the physical body, and the higher self has already retrieved a new aspect of light from the oversoul. The first thing the higher self will do is take the new aspect through a review process, looking at every necessary detail of your life. The new aspect will learn of all of your friends, relatives, and potential relationships—all of the things that you have said and done, along with all of the great essences of light that you have become aware of. Once the new aspect has been thoroughly schooled in the entirety of your essence, the exchange can proceed.

The exchange happens in the minutest microseconds of illusionary time processing. The exchange takes place so quickly that neither of the two aspects is fully aware of when the process begins and when it ends. All they know is that a new emergence of energy has begun to take place. What happens next is the entirety of the cellular memory is brought into alignment; it is settled in very calmly and opened into its own new world.

What has happened is that the matrix energy force within each and every cell of the physical body caused the cells to duplicate themselves, much like that of the DNA world. Each cell then split apart into two pieces, creating a mirror image. That mirror image was then utilized to accept the light of the new aspect. The mere step of accepting the new light within each cell fed it into both aspects at the same time, thereby simultaneously releasing the original aspect back to the higher self. At that point, the two energies collapsed back onto each other and the walk-in process was complete.

One of the most interesting things about this is that the cellular consciousness has to be completely reprogrammed. The entirety of the thought process of the system which you call the left brain has to be expanded into all possibilities, until the right brain can coordinate all of the possibilities. Then the right spectrum of the brain examines each cell carefully to make sure that each cell is in the same exact proportion as it was prior to the transfer. All this together creates the magnetic gridlines which establish the circuitry of the entire physical embodiment.

Once that is done, all energies feed back to the brain spectrum. Then the information received by the brain realigns the heart, or core presence, to vibrate at a new level discernible only by the higher self. When this is complete, the whole body then shifts into the next level of awareness. All is first remembered in perfection and then set into motion. In this process, the new aspect becomes aware that it has taken on human form.

All that I have just described takes place in less than 1/1000th of one second. So you begin to understand how rapidly energy can pulsate through the system called the body when it is in its released form of light, meaning that it is not conjured in thought but totally released in the light of experience. That, my friends, is one of the very beautiful things about being in your matrix. You are allowed the different possibilities to experience, and when you have no longer the need, the higher self has another plan. We have something called the Shift, and for that, you will move to the next light.

Walk-Ins at the Shift

How is the Great Shift affecting the walk-in process at this time?

KIRAEL: It is now becoming more of a process where only those willing to stay the Shift with bodies in pretty good shape will maintain them. Those not wanting to go through the Shift while still having good, strong body processes are usually making agreements with their higher selves to be replaced by other aspects.

Walk-ins, you must understand, are completely renewed subjects, so to speak. In essence, your higher self and another higher self make an agreement whereby your higher self releases your light presence, allowing your physical body to be utilized by another. The transfer between the two higher selves is not 100% complete because your higher self must maintain a connection to you, the originating aspect that holds the memories and feelings of the past. At the same time, your higher self definitely releases its controlling energy focus to that new spark of light that has taken over, that new aspect maneuvering in the physical world in your body.

Walk-Ins and Their Blueprints

What happens to the original blueprint when a walk-in takes place?

KIRAEL: A walk-in process literally involves lifting out the old blueprint and replacing it with the new blueprint—with the exception of four memory chromosomes. These four memory chromosomes are from the original blueprint and contain full memory of what was before the walk-in process took place.

Walk-ins Come Later in Life

Can walk-ins come in at a very early age?

KIRAEL: Walk-ins can come in any time, post-birth. It does not happen in the birthing channel because there is too much of a connection to the mother, but it can happen any time after that. Most walk-ins, however, take place at a much later time in life.

The Walk-In was the Higher Self

Once in a meditation I felt the whole left side of my body get rewired while the right side remained the same. For a period of time after that I felt

really fluid on the left and almost wooden on the right. Can you explain that process?

KIRAEL: Well, my friend, you know that the body functions on what are called magnetic grids. Those magnetic grids are polar, if you will, in their own generation. What that simply means is that the magnetic grids run the full length of your processing unit, your body. In running the full length of the body system, they have attunements aligned to the vibration of the system that is being replaced.

In your case, your impression of who you were then and who you are now seems to be completely regenerated. The simplistic explanation is that you received what would be considered a form of a walk-in. Listen carefully because this is uncommon over here: your higher self decided to re-aspect itself, not by bringing in a full walk-in or another energy pattern, but by bringing into your system more of its own core essence.

In cases such as yours, the whole body is not capable of accepting the full awareness, so only one half can enter your vibratory system at a time. In simple terms, your higher self "aspected" itself at the purest of levels and decided that it would take you to the next journey by implementing its own reality inside of what it already was. Instead of allowing for a walk-in, where one gets another training lesson, your higher self created a situation whereby you could raise your vibration in tune to the Fourth Light. This process, now partially completed, will be fully integrated when the dimension of the Earth matches the vibration of your system.

Now I must tell you, my friend, that throughout those times, you would sometimes despair while you tried to understand who you were compared to who you are. Yet I will tell you now, my friend, you are who you have always desired to be. You have brought forth that pattern of energy that has come from the high mastery levels, and in that, you will see that deservedness as it opens into its own force. You are more your higher self. And that is truly uncommon, my friend.

So as your higher self finds its fullness, which is probably about the time the Earth plane finds its shifting process, you will become aware of what it feels like to be a higher self incarnated into a human body; in part living here, in part living there. For now, the only thing that you might concern yourself with is maintaining the connection between the two so that you may travel back and forth between the different realities. But you will find soon that there is here, and here is where you want to be.

Splinters are Not Multiple Personalities

I have heard of the phenomenon of multiple personalities and of the colors of eyes changing when different personalities appear. Is that in any way related to the splinter aspect?

KIRAEL: Not necessarily so. Instead, that is usually the higher self having, shall we say, a "grander controlled aspect." What that means is that the higher self is taking a very active role with the part that you consider human. In truth, when the higher self has full awareness of its own inner light, it may allow one of its individual aspects to experience other personalities that it had in other lifetimes. As opposed to there being a number of aspects in one body, a number of life fragments are operating within the same vibrational system. The result can be a great amount of confusion, along with a breakdown in communication within that person, causing both the eye coloring and skin pigmentation to change. In such cases, the higher self will try to bring focus to the confusion, although the situation is very difficult to reverse once started. Usually the process will play itself out until one part becomes dominant.

Healing and Schizophrenia

Is schizophrenia related to splinters, twin flames, or aspects?

KIRAEL: In the medical world, schizophrenia occurs in a person when there are two separate thought systems operating in an almost simultaneous fashion. From the world of Guidance, we view schizophrenia as a process which involves two aspects holding onto the same presence. For instance, there may be a glitch in the process and something stalls as one aspect is leaving and another is entering. The end result is that both aspects remain in the same body process. The only reason they are not in opposition to each other is because both are reduced to half their power.

The only way to resolve this situation is to nurture the predominant aspect. Once you nurture that aspect, the other weaker one will release its hold within the presence. Traditionally, the solution is to administer drugs and use confinement spaces to prevent the so-called schizophrenic person from being a problem to society.

Another alternative would be to focus the light onto the more dominant aspect and hold truth to it. In other words, not let go of it, but heal it. Then the light of healing would interweave through the energy force, helping the schizophrenic person resettle his or her energy. By directing healing to the more dominant aspect, the weaker aspect would lose its force. It would automatically release itself from the body and return to the higher self. Yes, going through this process can be quite traumatic; however, the end result will find the person dealing with only one journey.

My son suffers from schizophrenia and is on medication, which definitely makes a difference in his personality, good and bad. I am wondering how the healing would occur. Is it by talking or is it by energetic transference?

KIRAEL: To heal schizophrenia, my friend, requires the combination of working on all four bodies simultaneously. When the medium worked with a young girl dealing with schizophrenia a while back, he had to focus the healing on all levels simultaneously. This involved mind melding and other healing processes that would leave him extremely tired at the end of a healing session. Indeed, the healer's state of exhaustion is because they begin to shift not only the physical world, but also the emotional, the mental and the spiritual worlds of the person, all at the same time.

Therefore, to address your question concerning medications, I would suggest that you try to reduce the drugs as much as possible because it is difficult to work with the altered state that the drugs create. In that state of mind, a person does not have the functionary awareness of its higher self. So whenever you can, limit the amount of drugs to a point where your son can establish a balanced state of mind. At the same time, you must understand that the balance will not last; it is only there long enough for you and others surrounding your son to help him find his way through the threshold.

Remember also that the balance is induced by drugs and can therefore be monitored only in the 10% mind, not in the spirit world. The 90% mind is where the play between the two aspects is actually occurring. So when drugs are used, you find that they tend to deprive the 90% mind of its active status, making the situation *appear* stable. The truth, however, is that the situation will not hold. You must work with the actual co-contributors by strengthening the predominant aspect and moving the other one out.

Closing Statement

Once again, I would suggest that you revert back to the chapter on the Four Pillars of Conscious Creation. For it is with the Four Pillars of Conscious Creation that you will know how to control all aspects of your life. The aspects of which we are speaking—the possibilities of higher selves and all of the processes that began as one light of God Creator—have all defined themselves solely in the best interest of your potential outcome.

Once you realize that you *are* the potential outcome—having the utmost ability to focus every aspect of your attitude, you will see with great clarity that your life is but a series of unfolding processes. When you experience the love of yourself, you give unto yourself the Light of Creation. This, in turn, allows you the human to experience the fullness of the journey that you have laid before you. When you recognize your ability to understand and create through your own soul energy experiences, you will know that you are a Light of Creation. You exist within the existence. You are the totality of existence.

Good evening.

9 9-11:
A WAKE-UP CALL FOR
LIGHTWORKERS

The September 14, 2001 "Evening with Kirael" live channeling session took on a tone of urgency in the wake of the airline hijackings and terrorist attacks on the World Trade Center in New York City and the Pentagon in Washington, D.C. on September 11, 2001.

Opening Statement

KIRAEL: Good evening.

This is a grand turnout we have this evening, isn't it? I would like to move right into the evening, for there is no time to waste in this third-dimensional illusion of time. It is a wondrous time, my friends, for it is a time for everyone who has the possibilities of awakening to exist within their own light. Indeed, it is now time to find the journey that best works for each person's own essence.

The Earth plane has definitely decided to create the Shift process that I have been speaking about for a number of years now. And it is time for you, the Lightworkers, to listen. I can only assume by your presence here this evening that you must be counted in that number. If you feel that you are not of the Lightworkers' reality, then what I shall say this night may be very difficult for you to hear. What I shall say will not be the rhetoric you have been hearing over the last few days; it will be clear and concise communications from another world, from one who watches over your plane in the most respectful light. We sit never in the judgment of light; we only know to expect endings and to understand that the light unfolds in many magical ways.

The Great Shift is On

Before speaking with you this night, I asked my medium to name our topic to fit with those who will hold the "swords of light," for you will be outnumbered greatly, my friends. There will be many that hold swords of steel, and many will hold the swords with barrels from which emanate great blasts, claiming the lives of many before they are through. Yet, there will always be the adventure, the thrill of being the soldier of light, the one who carries the light sword like that of Master Jesus. And that will be the quest of many now, for they have come to an understanding that what has taken place is just too bizarre for the human mind to contemplate.

My friends, listen to me carefully, as I name a few places that shall ring truth in your light. It shall ring of a time in your not-so-distant history, when a young man with a tiny mustache under his nose created havoc and spurred the world into a whole new awareness. Hundreds of thousands of your brothers and sisters died at that time so that we would never let that happen again to the Earth plane. Let's bring it closer up in history as well, to a time about sixty years ago, when opposing forces forgot that they were brothers and sisters of the world. They brought great devastation to this island [O'ahu] where you sit this night where death was just a part of that December 7 day until it was only a memory, and the world suffered. It suffered greatly in those times of which I have spoken.

And there are many other times, my friends, when devastating things have happened on your Earth plane and people have left this Earth by the thousands. Now, we have it on our doorstep once again. However, let me share with you the difference between then and now. It is not likely that anyone in this room saw the horrible camps in Nazi Germany. Not many in this room watched the airplanes fly from the sky and heard the cries of the young men jumping over the sides of the ships into a burning hell in Pearl Harbor. But many of you have now witnessed the devastation just three days ago—you have witnessed it with your own eyes. You have watched on your television screens a full-size airplane slam into the side of a building. Admit it, aren't you truly unsettled?

It is not hard to believe that you would be unsettled and angry, because you live in a society that is based in fear. What fear? It is the fear that you have lost something that you cannot regain. I say to you, my friends, not only *can* you regain what you have lost, but I assure you, you *will* regain it. You will have to pay a heavy price by the looks of things because you are not as prepared for this shift process as we had hoped you might be. We had hoped by now, in the second year of the new millennium, that we would be ready to do the Shift. We were praying that all of the human world would be ready. We haven't quite made it.

So the devastation keeps coming, and we, the Lightworkers—you in the human world and I of the Guidance Realm—must now thoroughly unite our energies to bring forth a new focus. A focus that will demand that Light become the premise of your Earth plane. A focus that will remind you of your brothers and sisters. A force that will bring you to the understanding that the God Creator is not some far-off essence, but one that exists within each and every one of you. A focus that reminds all of you that you are part of this beautiful Creator Light. And that no matter what has taken place, no matter how you see it as devastating, your life will go on. My friends, you must open up your hearts now. You must find it within yourselves to choose to let your light shine within, for in that, the world has a chance of existing.

Oh, this world will exist, my friends, for now there will be a large amount of Lightworkers that will cross over into the new Light. They will go with their light swords shining and gleaming before them. And each one that they touch with their light swords will brighten their own Light again, and they will hold fast to the truth that we are the Creator's Light.

The Shift That Didn't Happen

Oh yes. There is one other source of Light that came to your Earth plane. You will remember about 2000 years ago that a young man was born to the Virgin Mary. (And would you know that there are people who still want to contest whether or not Mary was a virgin? Not that it makes a grand deal of difference, but I would like to share with you that she surely was.) In any case, the young man, Jesus, was born onto the Earth. And as he became a man, he looked at the people around him, and he cried. He cried out to his Father and said, "What can I do here? There is so much malice. There is so much hate and discontent—so many people fighting about who belongs to You or how You belong to them, God." And the Creator looked down upon his beautiful son, and he said, "It is time, my beautiful son. It is time to walk to the river and meet your brother, your brother of light." And Jesus obeyed, and he walked to the river.

On that day, Jesus stood on the riverbank and saw a certain young man dunking the people under the water and screaming out at the top of his lungs, "You are reborn! You are rebirthed! You are alive! Go with the God Creator, if you will!" So young Jesus stepped into the water and walked up to this young man, John. And he said to John, "Would you be so kind as to baptize me in that same Light?" John fell to his knees, and he said, "I cannot baptize you, my Lord. You are the one sent from God Itself."

Jesus walked from the river that day as a brand-new light, with but one desire in his heart. And that desire was to remind everyone that they were brothers and sisters in love, and to remind every single one of them that all could heal if they would but take the journey. Next, we fast-forward to a time that was so devastating for most all of you to remember—when this same man, so filled with Light, who came here to do so much, cut his journey short and ascended into the heavens.

Swords of Light

Well, my friends, the people who were in those giant buildings on 9-11, they all had their journeys as well. They all had their plans. And now, they serve us as light beings. Now they remind us that it is time to change. They remind us in our prayers; they remind us when we sleep and in our walking on the Earth. Every time we watch the events from that day on television, those light beings no longer in human form remind us that we are to pick up our swords of light like the ones they carried. And I assure you, they now walk amongst us.

Just like your beautiful Jesus, every person that died for no apparent reason in Washington, in New York, and in those airplanes now knows why he or she died. It is for the highest purpose of all that we are reminded that no longer can we become complacent and forget that these horrid things can happen. Now we see them like never before, and now, we will take action.

In the last three days, my friends, the number of Lightworkers has almost doubled from where it was a week ago. Most of you don't even know what that means. Most of you think "So what? Big deal." I tell you something, my friends, when I say "almost double," it is almost enough to get us to the Shift now. It is almost enough to take us home into the Light and still maintain these physical bodies that you have. It is, as many here have said, an exciting time, indeed.

So when you next say your prayers, say them to every one of those light beings that not so many days ago were like you, in flesh and blood, wondering what the next day was going to bring or what they would be doing later in their lives. Honor those who lost their lives on 9-11, for they are now light beings, many in the angelic forces, acting as the light presence to lead others through the Shift.

I hope you will accept this as an opening statement, for the words come from a space far beyond my own. They are the words dictated by a council that asked me to be their spokesman. It is a council that works very closely with your Earth plane.

I have come to you this night to answer your questions. I do not hail from your Earth plane, so I cannot always answer your questions as you might want. I promise you, however, that with every ounce of my light, I will answer them as you need to hear them. That said—if anyone is in the modality to break free of the meditative state that they find themselves in, please simply step over to the microphone and we can begin our evening of questions.

Questions & Answers

Sending Angels, Light and Healing Energy

Good evening. I would like your guidance, please, on how best to help. I know how to hold love, but beyond that, is there any more help that you can give us?

KIRAEL: Yes. I would offer you this, my friend. In all sincerity, there are those who are capable of running into Manhattan now and throwing aside bricks and doing all that is humanly possible to do. They can do all of the mental work, and all of the emotional crying, besides the physical work, of course. But for you, who cannot go in person, you must realize that your job is as important as the jobs of those digging in the rubble today. You must know that it is important for you to go there at every opportunity in another way—as the Lightworker. It is important for you to send your higher self, and to pray that your angels go there, and that they be of service to the injured and to those who no longer have existence on this plane.

If that isn't enough for you in the Lightworkers' world, would you be so kind to also send your angels to visit your President—his name is President Bush. And I state this to you in emphatic energy because of what the medium told me. He told me that just recently your President stood in front the cameras and a reporter said to him, "You can say all you want about the things that are to be done, but what does your heart say?" And your young President got a bunch of tears in his eyes, and they rolled down his cheek, and he had to take a breath. Don't you feel a little bit better about your President nowadays? He needs all the light you can give him so that he doesn't make any harsh mistakes.

What else can you do? You can bring your light higher than you have ever brought it before. You can have faith in your healing powers as you have never had before. Because I will tell you something, as we speak, there is more healing needed in New York City than in any other place in the world. And it isn't just for the firefighters and the policemen and the people that are below the rubble, but it is for the people making sense of their lives again.

And you, being a long-distance healer, along with all of my long-distance healing friends, can work many hours a day, every day of your week, to send light there for whoever is in need of it. Your job is bigger than anyone else pulling rocks off the pile, my friend. You are a healer and you know what you must do. You know that now is the biggest test that you have ever faced because this isn't a test of trying to prove anything to anyone. This is a test of doing it. And you will pass, my friend. This I know because you have the soul that journeys with the healers.

That is the best answer I can give you, my friend.

"Miss Liberty"

I had a dream at 4:00 a.m. on Tuesday morning, which is the time that the tragedy happened in New York City. My dream was that I was supposed to research the name of the new Statue of Liberty, and the secret was held with a scientist named Anakan. She either knew the name or how to get the name. Then I woke up. So I was wondering if there was a message or anything that I needed to know?

KIRAEL: There is, my friend. And while the answer may cause many people within the audience to smile, this may not be an occasion for a lot of smiling (although I don't mind if you do). You did not have a dream Tuesday morning; you had an experience. And the experience was that they drew you home for just a moment. They drew you home. Now, a lot of people don't know of your Sirian background, my friend, but your Sirian brothers and sisters drew you home to a place where they held a grand meeting. And there, they said that they wanted someone to scribe their inner thoughts.

Their thoughts were, "We have need for one of us on the Earth plane to watch it [the 9-11 event] from on far, and to feed the energy back to us so that we will see it as a human would see it. And we will note it in all annals of time. This is something that we will show throughout the galaxies, throughout the cosmos. We will show it to all the incoming energies so they will know that the Earth plane has hit its latest devastation. It is now time to help repair it."

What you have said about renaming the Statue of Liberty, my friend, is that there was to be great disaster brought upon the Statue of Liberty, but the guides and the angels protected her. So she now needs a new name; she needs to be known as Liberty, Miss Liberty. You will understand more when you return to your crafts of light.

Who Did It?

Hello. I want to ask a more third-dimensional question. Was bin Laden behind the attack on the World Trade Towers?

KIRAEL: I hesitate to answer questions that would put my medium in very grave danger. I will say this, however, because I am compelled to answer any question asked of me: When you look in that direction, you have looked the very closest that you will ever be able to look into the eyes of darkness, and they will be spelled in the same way his name is.

The Line Has Been Drawn

Did this recent event further the cause or the agenda of the New World Order? In other words, did 9-11 speed things up a bit, thus giving many people the opportunity to be preparing for the Shift?

KIRAEL: I would answer the question this way, my friend. I would suggest to you that the line has been drawn in the sand. You are either going to be part of the dimmed energies of the over-mastermind, which is the collective fears of the Earth matrix, or you are going to step forth into the light. If you step into the light, you will begin to emerge like that of a beautiful rose in blossom. You will get stronger and stronger, instead of weaker and weaker, no matter what the over-mastermind has in store for you. The Lightworker is now on the other side of the line, and there the light is going to shine until it gathers as many Lightworkers to it as it can. Then, the world truly begins to make its shift, and you are part of it.

Chaos in Creation

I know that I am of the dragon world, but before that I originally came from the Guidance Realm and I was an angel child. What happened with my world was the forces that were angry against the Creator destroyed my light realm. Since then I have had to live with the pain of my lost world. I was wondering if the same forces that destroyed my world—the over-mastermind you spoke of—are the same forces that are causing the grief people are experiencing at this time.

KIRAEL: My friend, I would like to preface my answer by saying I am honored that you would have the courage to speak these words, because there are those who will hear them and think, "Whoa, where is she coming from?" You are coming from other worlds that they don't understand. Truly, they don't. Your world most assuredly was devastated and completely obliterated long before anything like time existed.

In answer to your question, every formation of life that is created has woven within it an element of chaos. It is literally woven into the etheric fabric so that you, the human being, or whatever being that might be present, could utilize that chaos to grow to their highest light potential. Understand that all must realize that every light has chaos woven into it. It is the Lightworkers who will create the space for the chaos to be diminished and the light to proceed.

Thank God, my friend. Thank the Creator that in this case the element of chaos is not the same one that obliterated your world of origination. For if it was, there likely wouldn't be enough Lightworkers to stop it. In this case, what I refer to as the over-mastermind, that of the dimmed energy, or that of chaos, is not as strong as the one you had to fight last time. My friend, you will know when it is time for you to pick up your sword again. But remember, the one time you tried to do it with the sword of steel, you lost your world. This time, use your sword of light and you will not lose.

"An Eye for an Eye" Or the Light

I ask this question because a lot of us are probably encountering similar situations. Soon after the events on Tuesday, I began an e-mail correspondence with somebody who I am quite close to. This someone is speaking of revenge, of war, and is focused on the negativity of the situation. I am wondering if you can help us to know what to say to people looking for revenge and focusing on the dark side. How can we bring our light swords to bear here?

KIRAEL: What a grand question, and what a great opportunity you have given me to answer. The answer, though, will not be loved by all, but the Lightworkers will understand. The little girl who spoke ahead of you knows exactly what I mean.

There have been those who have taken out their swords of metal and have crashed out into the etheric fabric. They have taken on everything possible and they have escalated it until there was nothing left to escalate—until the enemy ate the enemy and there was nothing but one enemy left to starve to death. That sounds vile, does it not?

Well, my friends, the answer that you must give to your friends who have the hatred gleaming from their eyes—and believe me, there are many more of them than there are of you. The answer you must give them is no answer at all. You must simply pray for them. You must simply nod your head in understanding because if you oppose them, you will find their wrath upon you, for those that speak of revenge have not the sense to calm their light. Don't tell them they are wrong; simply make sure that you never fall prey to their negativity.

Make sure that you, the Lightworkers, hold the light. Send a beam with a beautiful pink or green light. Do it very gently. Do not raise your hands to send it to them because they will get upset with you. Just hold the vigil, my friends. Hold the vigil and gather every Lightworker that you can. And tell your friends, one at a time, that your heart is stable, that your heart is ready to move into the light.

If someone must be punished, as stated in the Bible, "an eye for an eye; a tooth for a tooth," well then, so be it—if that be their journey. You will only know when the journey is complete, but say not to them that they must change. Say not to them that they must pray. Say not to them anything. Simply nod your head and listen to them. Maybe, just maybe, the venom that they need to vent will be vented on you. You will then gather it up in a loving ball of light, and you will hand it off to one of your angelic friends and say, "Here. Please take that out of here. We don't need it anymore."

I hope this answer will get you through this process with the least amount of turmoil possible.

Lemuria's Essence in New York

My question has to do with a little story that I would like to relate. The story is that I went camping at Ka'ena Point last Sunday night with a companion. When I got there, I felt a really strong sense of death all around, literally. Where we were camping is held by ancient Hawaiians as one of the places here on O'ahu where spirits leave the island. And, in fact, I sensed death all around and kept getting images of giant birds, and of people running. Then in the middle of the night, I woke up for no apparent reason. I also woke up my friend and we talked about what I had been experiencing. I asked what time it was and he said that it was 3:48, which is apparently the time that the World Trade Center was hit. We talked for a few more minutes and then I said, "Well, that feeling has passed. It's gone. Everything's okay now. It is clear." Having no radio with us, we knew nothing about any of what had taken place in New York until we returned home.

My question is, what does all this have to do with me personally? And as for this being Lemuria, the land of Mu, and Ka'ena Point, does it all fit together somehow?

KIRAEL: It is easy enough, my friend, especially if you are from the Seventh Light, which I am.

You ask what does it have to do with you personally. It means that you were literally sent to Ka'ena Point, you and your traveling companion, although you had no idea of why you were to be there. But then again, those people that were sent aboard those airplanes had no idea why they were there, either.

You were sent to Ka'ena Point to lie out there beneath the stars. That which you experienced in the first part of the evening as death and of a great bird flying was Lemuria opening her light and sending it to where it was going to be needed the most. The time of 3:48 a.m., when you awoke, is when all the light energy had left and the island was to be held by you, the Lightworkers. It was as though Lemuria would be "soul-less" for the next few hours.

You see, the Guides and the Guardians of Developmental Societies knew that there were enough Lightworkers on this particular planet, or this particular island called O'ahu, that they could send forth all of their beings of love and light. So what felt as though the beauty of Lemuria was dying was, in fact, Lemuria resetting its energies. All the Lightworkers that woke up between the hours of 2:00 a.m. and 6:00 a.m., for whatever reason, were awakened to hold the light of this island. For the love of this island had gone to New York to be of assistance to what was about to happen there. [For more information on the Guardians of Developmental Societies, please see *Kirael Volume II: The Genesis Matrix*, Chapter 1.]

The Light Sword

I am trying to figure out what to do with the light sword. You have taught us a lot about the tools for the Shift, and I am sensing that that this is another of our tools, but I don't know what to do with it. When I think of a light sword, I think of Luke Skywalker in "Star Wars" and the buzzing sound of his sword as he wielded it in the movie. What do we do with ours?

KIRAEL: Many of the light swords are just that way. You can actually hear them *whir* when you extend them. Yes, there is a *whirring* sensation. But let me tell you something. Most of the Lightworkers need to hold their light swords in tightly to them so that the tip of the sword is found in the palm of their hand, and the rest of it runs up their arm and attaches to their heart. You see, the light sword is an extension of the Lightworker's arm.

Here is a really good idea. When you lay your hand upon somebody's shoulder, just reach out and pull them close to you. Let the *whir* go, and you will feel them shift. For those people that you cannot physically touch with your hands, let your light sword extend out of your hand. For example, if you come upon a crowd of people who are unruly and aggravated, let your light sword extend and just wave it over them. Let them feel the vibration. Some will feel it, some won't, my friend.

An Impassioned Lightworker Speaks

This is one of those times when I find it hard to explain why bad things happen to good people, and I find myself saying, "All right. So what was the reason for this?" I was angry when it happened, but I didn't find myself directing my anger towards any particular religion or ethnic group. I mean, that is ridiculous. That has nothing to do with it.

My wife said, "Why are you angry?" And I said, "Well, there is a group of very dark forces at work here, and they are using these people in a last desperate attempt to prevent the Shift from happening. I am afraid that they will strike such fear into people that people will be willing to give up some of their freedoms in order to achieve what they consider to be security." And sure enough, the question that I am hearing repeatedly is, "Well, what freedoms are we willing to give up at this point?" Hearing that has made me so angry because I finally understood the real aim of the attack. The attack was to instill such fear in us that we would give up the freedoms we have for a false sense of security and protection.

There is a quotation of Benjamin Franklin that actually addresses that idea. His words in effect were that those who are willing to consider giving up freedom for a measure of security deserve neither their freedom nor their security. I loved it; I thought it was well put. As for the group of people who attacked the World Trade Center, they are in some last desperate attempt. I think the people behind the scenes have managed to do just the opposite of what they intended. Rather than dividing the people, I think they have actually managed to unite them. Do you believe that?

KIRAEL: My friend, with the beautiful speech that you just made, don't expect to get on CNN. They don't like people talking like you. You stop it right now or you will not get on television. [*laughter*] Sorry. I couldn't resist saying that because it is the truth.

I will answer your question in this light. There is a force behind the force. As you know by my answer to an earlier question, I will not endanger my medium. But I will come this close by telling you that the force behind the force is going to surprise all of you. The ugly little head will rear itself and you will get to see it. And when you do, you are all going to wish that you had taken an even stronger stand in light because that is when you will discover that all you have is the light. Light is the only thing you have, my good friend. It is what you have to carry you through the whole process, and to take a stand. Yes, I am so glad you honestly admitted your anger, but I can also see your wife's beautiful face as she smiled up at you and said, "Who are you?"

Children are Holding the Light

I would like for you to address the children. As a teacher, I am not seeing the kinds of behaviors I expected to see as a result of the 9-11 tragedy. Some of the children were very matter-of-fact about what took place. They asked some questions, but I didn't see the fear that I was expecting. I have also been very watchful of my own fifteen-year-old son, and it has been the same response. Interestingly, I found myself needing to be hugged and told that everything was all right. So, what is going on for the children? I tend to think that they are helping the adults through this experience.

KIRAEL: I will speak to that most gladly, my friend.

The fifteen-year-olds and younger are able to cope with this situation much better than the adults. This is because you of the adult world are hearing things such as, "You have lost your way," and "You have lost your light." Or you are hearing that you are no longer whole and that you have been raped and pillaged, so to speak. And you know what the children are saying? "It didn't hurt me." And you know what? It really didn't hurt them, as you would imagine. They are also aware that they need to hug the older folks every now and then because you are all rattled up. They want to bring the light onto the Earth plane. This is why they don't get so excited. They don't throw themselves into the terror the way the adult world has—because they understand.

So here is the answer to you and your children, and the children of your children, for they will one day come to be. In this very moment, the children are the light force of the Earth plane, and you in the adult world should take a long, hard look at the vast majority of them. It is not as though they are cold and calculating. It is just that they know that there is a process going on, and they may not be able to verbalize it, my friend. They have little to say, other than how they interact with the process itself. So when they are out there by themselves without you adults hanging about them, they are saying things like, "Well, we got ourselves in a fix this time. We have a whole world of adults out there acting like kids, and we may have to act the part of the adult now. We must be strong."

That is what they are doing. Little kids, four and five years old, are putting their arms around their granddaddies and saying, "It is going to be all right, granddaddy. Don't worry so much. Don't cry like that." They speak like that because they know. They know that they are here for the Shift. They know the Shift will happen, and they are prepared for it. Now all we have to do is to get the adults in alignment with these young people, and the children know that. They are going to help you, my friend. Don't despair.

Cleaning Up the Rubble in a New Way

First of all, my heartfelt gratitude to you for sharing your wisdom with us. In the past three days it seems that all the things that you have been sharing with us about the Shift for the past ten years seem to fit together now. It seems like all the pieces fit. So from my heart, I just want to say thank you.

KIRAEL: Thank you for listening.

My question concerns the devastation and cleanup that seem almost humanly impossible to deal with. A while back you said that it would take galactic intervention to help us clean up Mother Earth. Is this one of those times that, if we start praying to the galactic energies, they will they help with the cleanup in New York City?

KIRAEL: Well, let's just say, my friend, that they sent *you* to help. I would ask each and every one who hears this recording or reads these words to imagine another scenario. Try to imagine a time when a group of people stood beside young Imhotep in ancient Egypt. Imagine that they had these great blocks of stone, and Imhotep said, "We are going to make a pyramid." And they looked at him and thought, "My God, there is no way. It will take us centuries to get these blocks built into a pyramid for you!" And Imhotep showed them a new way of doing things. Well, you on the Earth plane must recognize there is a new way of doing things. When you do, the rubble will clear up not only in Manhattan, but also around the world. There must be a new way of doing things, don't you think?

So search, yes, for your galactic brothers and sisters, and for your angelic presences and guides such as I. Listen to the words on a more careful note, and you will understand that there is a new way of doing things. Now is the time to put all that you have learned into practice.

Please listen, not just you, but all of you. I know that you can tell me, "Oh, I am meditating. I pray." Well, because you are still telling me this, I have questions about it. When you stop telling me and show me, then I will know the world is a safer place to live in. Let yourself *be* that one, my friend.

Let yourself open up your heart and show the people how it is done by your own performance. Don't tell them how to do it. Don't tell them you are doing it. Don't shout from the rooftops. Show them the light and then the rubble goes away.

Shining Light on the Over-Mastermind

I am a little nervous about this question and I don't know why. Yesterday in my private session with you, you mentioned that this disaster created a wave of thought forms around the world and that is why a lot of us felt sick. Well, it started me thinking, because I have been seeing a grid that is really close to the surface of the Earth Mother and another one further out around the Earth. I am wondering if we as Lightworkers can start affecting the over-mastermind by joining together to send energy through the grid.

KIRAEL: You absolutely can, but be prepared. A few minutes ago, I spoke with my little dragon lady friend who experienced major changes to her world. I don't know if she will remember or not, but she experienced a time when the forces of her world decided to readjust and realign the grid at too harsh of a pace. What happened was that they lit it up so brightly that the over-mastermind literally exploded on them. So I say, yes, yes, and yes to those of you that can see the grid now, but do it discerningly with your light particles.

Here is the most important thing I say to you. If you are going to become a grid worker, and many of you are, normally the grid will look like columns of numbers. Look for the cross-section that seems to have a gap between it and the one above it. This is the weakest space of the grid. In between those spaces is where the over-mastermind is aligning its energy.

So if you use your light, especially your light swords, and you cleanse that area, the over-mastermind will lose its grip. Here is the most beautiful thing I will say to you, my friends. If the over-mastermind loses its grip, it won't fight with you. It will fight with itself for life. And when this happens, you will walk through this thing like a hot knife in a big chunk of butter. That is how quickly you can do it.

What I have seen look like little rips or tears in the grid. Is that right?

KIRAEL: That is right.

Thank you.

KIRAEL: All right. The answer that I just shared could bring the energy of the over-mastermind to an end.

An Eye to the New Reality

Here is a question from a reader of the "Kirael Shift Reports" in

Tallahassee, Florida. The first question refers to Tara's statement in Chapter 8 of "Kirael Volume II: The Genesis Matrix," that "the world will appear unsuitable for human life if viewed with the physical eyes." Will the third eye be used following the Shift to truly see the beauty of the new reality?

KIRAEL: I will answer it in this fashion. Right now, most of your sight is with your regular eyes; therefore, most of you are seeing a dimension that you don't really want to be part of. But when you use your third eye and see the possibilities of existence and of a world that could come to a much higher vibration, then you begin to see clearly. Post-Shift, you will use your third-dimensional regular eyes only for the fun of it, while the vast majority of your sight will be done with the third eye.

"Who" is the Over-Mastermind?

Although this person's question was emailed prior to 9-11, it remains relevant to the events that have just taken place. He would like to know "who" the planetary masterminds are that deter us at every corner.

KIRAEL: Ooh, he would like me to name them, just as another person already tried to ask earlier? Is that what he is asking?

Well, he has "who" in quotes.

KIRAEL: All right. Well, that was a good try, too.

I will answer it this way, and it actually is a grand answer when you think about it. "Who" is the energy that many of you have contributed to. "Who" is that thought that you have held in your mind. "Who" is also that somebody you have been angry with and have held that anger against for a day or so. Every part of that anger contributed to the over-mastermind by giving it strength to keep its dim light active. "Who" is all the Lightworkers who have just become Lightworkers—those, who before they were Lightworkers, cursed out their brothers and sisters of the universe, who spent more time being angry than in love.

That is the "who," my friend. It is those that have fed the over-mastermind that makes it feel as though it is empowered to do whatever it wants. But I will tell you something. "Who" is also going to break it apart, because they are waking up in the same light.

Is This President Bush's Awakening?

Good evening. I feel compelled to humbly thank you for all the help you have given souls in their transformation. I, too, have felt it.

In regards to President Bush, you said some months ago something to the effect that a higher part of him, or the best part of him, would come forth if others didn't get to him first. It appears that that has been happening. I believe you said that in an earlier session.

KIRAEL: The statement was that you have a good President—if he didn't get taken over by the over-mastermind which has controlled most of his external life. He made a commitment into the light force before he was made your President. The commitment he made was that one day he would work on the side of the Lightworker without the over-mastermind and the rest of the world even knowing it.

And I also stated unto you that when he awoke, there would be devastation upon Earth. Well, the devastation is here, my friend, and so is his awakening. I believe in my heart that if we can hold enough light on him, the over-mastermind may have lost this one, and the Lightworkers will have gained one.

The Numbers 9-1-1

I want to thank you for doing this, for being here, and for this place (the Honolulu Church of Light), because we need it.

This evening I didn't know what I was going to ask you until I stood in line. I only knew I had to get in line for some reason and that part of my question had to do with numbers.

For a very long time in my life I have been plagued by the number 9-1-1 and also the reverse, 1-1-9. I have had license plate numbers and at least three addresses that were either 1-1-9 or 9-1-1. I have often had airline flights with these same numbers. To add to that, my sister, probably the dearest person to me on the planet, has also had many airline flights with 1-1-9.

I feel incredibly blessed that my sister and I came into the same family, because from a very early age we had some knowledge that we were from somewhere else and that we came here together. She is in town visiting me right now and was here on Tuesday, 9-11. She was supposed to leave today but couldn't because the airports are still closed for security reasons.

The medium knows of the things going on in my life and has helped me realize everything in my life is lining up. Everything is happening according to some order and it seems to be done ahead of time for me so that by the time I get there, it is already there. I would love any insight into these numbers, and about what my sister and I are to do in this extra-special time that we have together.

KIRAEL: Well, I would honor that question in this very fashion, my friend. And many of the people out there will resonate to my answer, but watch the faces of the crowd as I say this: 9-1-1 brings you to duality in terms of my numerology. [See Kirael's Numerology in *Kirael Volume II: The Genesis Matrix.*]

The reason you personally have been plagued by the 9-1-1 is because when you volunteered to leave the angelic corps and come to the Earth plane, you were volunteering to come into duality. And while you have enjoyed being here for the most part, you almost got lost in it until just recently, when you awoke to your own powers. As you awoke to your powers, my friend, it reminded you that you are not 9-1-1, but that you are one sent to guide 9-1-1 into the Shift of Light. That is why your sister has been held here for a few more moments in your light, so that you can be reminded of your love for her and hers for you. Very seldom can a brother and sister of the same soul family feel what the two of you feel.

So I suggest to you, my friend, that 9-11 is a grand awakening for you to remember why you have come here. It is here to remind you to be in light with the 9-1-1 and to help those who need the help. That you already know. Thank you for your honor of being here. If anybody reaches out and touches your hand when you walk back to your chair, don't be surprised.

Thank you, Kirael. I might add that my nametag tonight shows the number 19.

KIRAEL: Which in numerology brings you to the number 1, or G-O-D. Good evening, my friend.

That will be a tough one to follow, won't it?

Healing in a Trinity of Love

After the events of 9-11, I went to the heiau (an ancient Hawaiian place of worship) to do some healing work. I worked with the crystal there and it was a phenomenal event. While I was there, I also had the honor of spending a few hours playing with a little one-and-a-half-year-old girl. I received the blessing that day that children are playing as healers.

I would like to know how to create a trinity of energy made up of the cetaceans, the crystal world and the children, who still maintain a strong connection to their higher selves. How can we amplify the healing process of the anger that some people have as a result of the World Trade Center attacks?

KIRAEL: The answer might be a bit bland for some of our excitement seekers, but here it is anyway. The simplicity is that the child—especially one who is willing to share a few moments with you—is there to remind you that if you create a trinity with the crystal core of Mother Earth, the child and yourself, you will find the child within yourself. In so doing, you will awaken the core issues of your light until every crystalline particle in your body begins to vibrate into that new light. When that trinity is formed, the center core becomes love, and each is reminded that love is the journey. That is the trinity, my friend.

Unexpected Feelings

Thank you, Kirael, for blessing us with your presence again. I am not exactly sure why I am standing here or even if I have a question, but I would like to follow up on what my friend said earlier about her experience at Ka'ena Point.

I was her companion on that camping trip, and some of the feelings I have been going through since then have left me a little confused. I am not a visionary as my friend is, nor did I have the sense of impending death, but I did feel restless all that day. And we both woke up at the same time, at 3:48 a.m., which I understand was exactly the time the first plane hit the World Trade Center, (9:48 a.m., New York time). What was first interesting and later confusing about this was that we both felt this great sense of peace, almost a sense of joy.

Then after the special 9-11 meditation that the medium, Rev. Sterling, held the following day here at the Honolulu Church of Light, he asked me what I had seen and felt during the meditation. I was really speechless because despite all of the devastation and the feeling of dark energies in my visions while we were meditating, there was this feeling of joy. So when he asked me, I was reluctant to mention it. Then by the following day, I had this feeling that present in the rubble were also angels. And the angels were saying that all is not what it appears to be, and that everything is in perfection.

So I am hoping that this joy I am feeling is related to all that has happened. Yet, it also feels strange to have this simultaneous feeling of joy in spite of all the suffering and devastation. I wondered if you could share some words that would clear this up for me.

KIRAEL: You definitely won't get on CNN either. You don't stand a chance. [*laughter*]

I will clear it up for you this way. As I explained to your companion of that evening, what you were a party to will change your life forevermore. The living truth is that you were a party to the spirit of a beautiful Lemurian light that exited right from where you were. It exited to be part of the healing process.

If you could be in New York, you would see all of the little angels that are throughout the rubble, if you would just turn your eyes a little bit to the side and look. If any one of you could be there, you would see little flashes of light all around you because the angels are all there.

And this joy you are feeling, my friend, cannot be experienced by many because they would have had to have been there on the western point of the island, where very few people go, by the way. But there you were, and anybody else that might have been around you would have felt the same presence. You were blessed with Lemurian light that morning.

So I say to both of you, your lives will never be the same again. When you see these things happening in the world, you will feel a peace. That peace will burst and expand outward, touching the next person. You now carry a light within you that will change your life forever, my friend. You came and stood in line not knowing the question because there is no question. You came to hear an answer that doesn't exist, for you now know the universe of light exists within you. You now know you are a star child, and of that beingness, both of you can touch whomever you wish and there shall only be light. I hope you can understand the depths of your healing, my friend.

A Comradeship of Lightworkers

When a catastrophe like this one strikes, it seems that there are two things that occur in people: one is that it brings out anger, negative emotions and horrendous feelings. The other is that it brings out the best in people.

I am wondering what the key to healing is in light of this catastrophe. Is the key to focus on the dedicated people involved in the rescue efforts and on the thousands who are sending prayers? Is the key to focus on the positive side as opposed to the side that generates anger and other negative feelings?

KIRAEL: I tell you this: CNN is never going to set up a camera in this church!

Let me just say it to you this way. There is a comradeship of Lightworkers that bursts forth at a certain point in all devastation, during any times of great unrest. There is always the light of those who have come together to serve the greater good. For those who come to serve the greater good are the Creator's Lights themselves shining. Although those in the over-mastermind are also lights of the Creator, their lights are dim; they cannot see the Creator's Light clearly any more. Hence, when you feel what you feel and you see what you see, and when it all comes together in the spirit of camaraderie, it is as though the light has been polished to a higher vibration. And, yes, my friend, that is the corps of Light.

That is why you have been sent to the Earth plane. Your light is to touch those that come before you, and that is why you came here to ask that question—just to see if anybody else out there is listening. The interesting part is: I am going to make a bargain here with you. Before we leave this evening, you know what it is to bring the lights together. And now is the time to do the work. Now is the time to bring the Lightworkers to bear.

A Soul of Darkness

A very interesting question was raised this evening about this "darkened energy" force. Is the individual who is thought to be behind the attacks a master wizard?

KIRAEL: How do I put this in your light so you will understand it? Let me just say that he has practiced beyond the wizards. He went beyond what wizards would do, and therefore, became someone beyond the wizards.

I might add that there are few that go beyond the wizards who live any great length of life. By that, I don't mean simply in the Third Dimension. I mean that usually when they go beyond the light of the wizards, they no longer dwell in the light process. They learn all the evil and all the discontent. In essence, they sell their souls into the darkness itself. So when they are finished with that life, they are returned into the Creator's Light. And at that particular moment, they are dispersed, never to become whole again. They must wait for a journey beyond the waiting of time, until one day they can "particle-ize" themselves and start a new journey from the very beginning. They must wait until one day they can begin to rectify a remnant of love that lost the light and became dark.

The Truth about Hugs

I just wanted to share that whenever someone we know transitions, or dies, it is only then that we realize how much we take life for granted. At the funeral of my grandmother, I suggested that all who still have grandparents give them a hug. Oftentimes grandparents don't have much contact with the grandchildren, so they love to hold and hug their grandkids every chance they get. I also want to share that one person at our last Council meeting suggested that we try every day to say good morning to our spouses. Ever since then, I always say good morning to my wife. Thank you.

KIRAEL: And the answer to his question is this: When you open your heart to one another in the human world, you discover you are not human anymore, and in that, you are the truth.

On Master Kirael and Master Jesus

A reader of the "Kirael Shift Report" is asking, "Where did you, Master Kirael, and Master Jesus originate from? From which planetary system?"

KIRAEL: We do not exist in a planetary system; we exist in the Light of Creation. In order to reach the level of vibration that we have reached, we must have experienced all potential civilizations, all potential forms of light. When I say "potential," I say to you, my friend, we must exist in all possibilities. In order to arrive at the Seventh Light, we must have done all, including the mastery of mastery, and then we are allotted the experience of aiding the human world.

Closing Statement

In closing, I say that each of you has come here this evening to awaken to another level of awareness. Each of you has received the 9-1-1 call, and in that 9-1-1 call, each and every one of you will awaken to the level of your own choice. I suggest that there are lots of people who will receive recordings of this event. The words will be sent out around the world to as many as possible. So I challenge each who receives this message to listen to it, and then to share it with a friend whom you know will make a difference. We cannot let the anger and the darkness prevail. We must have the light be the one thing that we hold in our own truth.

My friends, there is but one Guardian Light, one God Creator in All That Is, and part of It resides within each of you. Don't let an act of a single being put your light out. Let your light shine brighter than ever before, for in that light you will recognize your light as Creation. Share this message with a friend that you trust to know who you are. In this way, they will discover you are a Lightworker. Together, united in light, we in the world of Light and you of the human experience must close the gap, for there is no separation between us.

Until we meet again, my friends, good evening.

CLOSING INSIGHTS

And the journey begins

It is clearly seen in this book that Kirael is guiding the human world to move us into higher levels of truth. He is ready to use every opportunity to show us that no limits exist. Until now, humans have been accustomed to acknowledging limits and living within those limits. Yet as we have seen here, we on the Earth journey can, and will, consciously create our own future.

In quantum physics, the mere act of viewing a particle under a microscope lens changes its life force forever. The same applies with our lives: the moment we can fully see and understand our lives, our lives are forever changed. Change is imminent.

Clearly, we are part of a wondrous new understanding that has no limits. We can have it all, and we can no longer use fear, or confusion, or feelings of less than as reasons not to move forward. Kirael has given us all the tools we need to explore a new life's journey.

In the next books in *The Kirael Collection*, be ready to travel to other realities beyond the human dimension. I have been there, often with Kirael as my guide. You are invited to join with us on a new adventure—to new, unseen worlds.

In the meantime, I know that my journey will be filled with many more awakenings. May it be the same for you. Together, hand in hand, we shall walk the path in the Creator's Light.

I hold you in the God Creator's Love and Light,

Rev. Fred Sterling

Honolulu Church of Light

Honolulu, Hawaii

2002

ABOUT THE AUTHOR

Reverend Fred Sterling is the Senior Pastor and Director of the Honolulu Church of Light. He is first and foremost a man of the heart, a healer, a person of unusual depth and contrast whose consciousness is rooted in the rich soil of life experiences.

At the Honolulu Church of Light, Reverend Sterling has emerged as a pioneering healer, author of *Kirael: The Great Shift*, *Kirael Volume II: The Genesis Matrix*, and *Guide to the Unseen Self*, host of a radio program and a weekly television program called "The Rev." With all this, he still holds truth that his most important role is that of medium for the wise and loving spiritual energy called Kirael, and through this, has touched the lives of many people around the globe.

Fred Sterling has embraced the adventure of life more passionately than even he thought possible. What validates his work as a minister, healer and author are precisely his life experiences. They have allowed him to cultivate a sense of candidness and authenticity. What you see is what you get; on the street or in a seminar room, his style is fully engaged and extemporaneous.

Fred Sterling is available for seminars, and for individual or group Kirael sessions.

For more information about the author and his work, visit *www.Kirael.com* or contact the Honolulu Church of Light at 1-800-390-1886.

THE KIRAEL COLLECTION

In the beginning there was one.

Soon there will be nine.

The Kirael Collection is a groundbreaking new compilation of channeled Kirael Sessions assembled by subject matter into a series of nine books.

Guide to the Unseen Self has been the first of these new books that challenge the mind to break free of the limits of space and time.

Wherever you are on your evolutionary path, a new portal of understanding awaits you. Join Kirael as he presents topics of extraordinary scope and cutting-edge relevance, topics that cross planetary and dimensional lines in exploring the universe within us and without.

Future topics:

Lemuria, Atlantis and the Great Shift – then and now

Galactics and Other Realities

Experience the wisdom and wit of Master Kirael in his endless compassion for the human experience on the planet Earth. If you've ever experienced a live session with Master Kirael through his medium Fred Sterling, you'll know that his knowledge is boundless in realities far beyond our own.

For order information, call us at 1-800-390-1886, or log on at www.Kirael.com

ALSO BY "THE REV" FRED STERLING
KIRAEL: THE GREAT SHIFT AND
KIRAEL VOLUME II: THE GENESIS MATRIX

What people are saying about these books:

"Kirael through Fred Sterling is right on! The Genesis Matrix is an empowering book filled with love and insight."

—**Lee Carroll—Best-selling new age author of the Kryon and Indigo Children Series of books**

"Rev. Fred Sterling brings a message of love and caring that removes dark places in the soul and gives hope. He awakens us to the experience that we can live our lives from the knowledge that we are connected to universal wisdom. He brings deep healing to all those who truly want to create inner peace."

—**Silke Vogelmann-Sine, Ph.D., Honolulu psychologist, author. New CD release: "Awakening...To the Reality That You Are Never Alone."**

"Reverend Fred Sterling is a man of integrity who can be trusted"

—**Robert Shapiro, professional channel, author of the Explorer Race Series**

"Kirael: The Great Shift is a fascinating read with valid and important information that is useful for the extraordinary frequency shifts that are occurring! I highly recommend it. I look forward to more from Kirael and Rev. Fred Sterling!"

—**Jonathan Goldman, author of "Healing Sounds," SHA Director, sound healing pioneer**

WANT MORE GUIDANCE TO YOUR UNSEEN SELF?

Let Kirael be your guide...

The Great Shift is here. Learn more about it with Kirael as your guide. The information is timeless in nature, yet fitting to the events that shape your life as the global shift in consciousness moves into high gear.

You can choose to play an extraordinary part in the awakening of the planet to the Shift or you can choose to endure as best you can the events that surround you. It is about choice.

Choose to be awakened. Join the thousands of Lightworkers who already have— then be on the leading edge of the Shift.

For the most current information on the Shift:

- Order and receive the FREE* Kirael introductory audiotape *"How To Have It All: The Ten Principles of Conscious Creation"* by calling 1-800-390-1886 or by ordering online at www.Kirael.com

- Subscribe to the *"Kirael Shift Report"* issued monthly via email** or in printed form

- Attend an *"Evening with Kirael"* live channeling session held monthly in the Honolulu Church of Light, Honolulu, Hawaii

- Listen to the audiotape recordings of *"Evening with Kirael"*

- Tune in to *"The Great Shift with Fred Sterling"* weekly Internet/ radio broadcast on Kirael.com

- Speak with Fred Sterling and Kirael, and guest Lightworkers on the broadcast

- Obtain your meditation, prayer and other "Tools for the Shift."

  See catalog that follows

- Be a part of the Kirael.com family – *where Lightworkers are amassing in love*

*With minimum shipping and handling fee of $4.50

**FREE OF CHARGE with membership to *Kirael.com*

See catalog on following pages
For more information, call 1-800-390-1886 or
visit *www.Kirael.com*

AUDIOTAPES BY KIRAEL
Recorded in Digital Stereo

How to Have It All: The Ten Principles of Conscious Creation—Ten-Tape Series
The Ten Principles of Conscious Creation are a series of simple but powerful tools that draw upon your inner knowing to create exactly what you intend. In this a ten-tape series, Kirael covers each of the Ten Principles of Conscious Creation: Truth, Trust, and Passion; Clarity, Communication, and Completion; and Prayer, Meditation, Sleepstate Programming, and Masterminding.
Item #7299-01A $69.95

The Ten Principles of Conscious Creation: Free Introductory Audiotape
This free introductory 90-minute audiotape is available for a minimum shipping and handling fee of $4.50. It is a prelude to the ten-tape set of Kirael's "How to Have it All: The Ten Principles of Conscious Creation." *Item #7299-01*

$ 9.95 each

Angels
The angelic realities are made up of soul love. They do not sit in judgment of you. They just chose to love you. Each of you has several angels working with you, helping to bring more Light into your life. Learn more of their importance on Earth for the Shift. *Item #7201*

Aspects and Splinters
To be in the Third Dimension, you must have made certain agreements to experience all that you desire to experience on the Earth plane. About every seventh year, you experience a shift in consciousness that is the result of a new part of your life plan (splinter) moving into place. This is all part of the evolution of your soul.
Item #7202

Christ Consciousness
Master Jesus came to the Earth plane with a beautiful message of healing through love. Oftentimes, the message has been drowned in a sea of noise. In this tape, Kirael reveals parts of Jesus' life seldom discussed today. *Item #7203*

Female Energies That Surrounded Christ
In the Bible there is very little mention of the female energies that surrounded Master Jesus. Kirael shares how the essences such as Mother Mary, Martha, Mary Magdalene and others, were in a position to greatly influence the historical events of that time. *Item #7204*

The Galactic Brotherhood
Please do not see them as a threat, because they are very peaceful and non-threatening and they have chosen to assist humanity through the Shift. The Sirians, Pleiadians, Andromedans and other galactic societies are here in our atmosphere. Each galactic society has a stake in the outcome of our post-Shift reality. *Item #7205*

The Great Shift
Every 2,000 years the Earth plane undergoes a shift in consciousness. Today, we stand at the doorway to a shift into the Fourth Dimension. Big changes are ahead. There is a raising of mass consciousness that will involve healing Mother Earth and the healing of self. Choose to move through the Shift in beauty and grace. *Item #7206*

Photon Energy
The greatest evolutionary event in history is Mother Earth's entrance into the Photon Energy that will take us into the Fourth Dimension. These events will bring changes that need not cause fear. Find out how the Photon Energy can be used to heighten manifestations through your love. *Item #7207*

Sharing Life With Your Ego
The ego is a very beautiful part of your evolution. The ego that you are so quick to judge is not as bad as you might think, for without it there would be no Third Dimension. The whole process is to learn how to heal the ego. Go beyond the ego and you will find your truth. *Item #7208*

Signature Cell Healing
Signature Cell Healing works with the Creator's essence in the body—the signature cell. This process allows the cellular clarity of the embodiment to awaken on all levels. It goes beyond the five senses and promotes healing in the etheric body— where there is no fear. *Item #7209*

Time Space–The Illusion
Time is an illusion. The space known as the "zone" is defined and measured by the brain. In the brain, there are pulses of energy. Between these pulses is a space where your true consciousness resides. Quantum Physics, New Time Physics, DNA, and more! *Item #7210*

Transitioning Into The Light
Kirael gives us insights into the process of completing a lifetime and transitioning into the Light. Keep an open mind as you listen to his profound wisdom, and allow your heart to open to a new level of awareness. *Item #7211*

Call 1-800-390-1886
or visit *www.Kirael.com*

"EVENING WITH KIRAEL"

Audiotape Recordings

Experience a monthly session with Kirael recorded live in Honolulu in digital stereo for only $10.00 each. Or get an annual tape subscription for $100 and receive two months free, shipping included!

I.D. #	*"Evening with Kirael"* 90-minute audiotape
7200S	*"Evening with Kirael"* audiotape subscription/one year
72-0001	Unmasking the Stranger in Your Relationships
72-0002	The New Church (Honolulu Church of Light)
72-0003	Warriors of Light
72-0004	The Awakened Dreams of Australia
72-0005	The May 5th Planetary Alignment
72-0007	Galactic Realities
72-0008	Existing Outside the Matrix
72-0009	Living Within the Matrix
72-0010	The Ancient Teachings of Tara: A Galactic Encounter
72-0011	Healing Karma
72-0012	The Origins of Christmas
72-0101	The Galactic Connection
72-0102	Passion: The Fire Within
72-0103	The Great Shift Update: Where Are We Now?
72-0104	Birth: Conception to the First Year
72-0105	The Journey from Lemuria to Atlantis
72-0106	Healing the Blueprint of Life
72-0107	Lemuria Falls and Atlantis Rises
72-0108	Galactic Interventions: Past, Present and Future
72-0109	9-11: Holding the Light Sword
72-0110	The Enchanting World of the Magi
72-0111	The Healing World of the Shaman
72-0112	Christmas with Kirael
72-0201	Prophecy 2002
72-0202	Dimensional Portals: Now or Later, Everyone Will Use Them
72-0203	The Lost Population of Mars
72-0204	The Crucifixion: A Spiritual Perspective
72-0205	Conversations With the Angels
72-0206	The 21st Century Male Liberation—Removing the Armor

To order the latest *"Evening with Kirael"* tapes or for further information, call toll-free **1-800-390-1886** Email: *ShopKirael@Kirael.com*, or order on-line at *www.Kirael.com.*

MORE AUDIOTAPES FROM KIRAEL

The Wisdom of the Lost Scrolls

Kirael narrates a series based on the ancient scrolls of the Alexandrian Library and presents insights that have never before been revealed.

Six 90-minute audiotapes $9.95 each
SPECIAL PRICE: Set of 6 for $47.95 Item #7212

This series includes:

The Mystery of Genesis
From the perspective of the Seventh Dimension, an amazing account of the beginnings of humankind on Earth. *Item #7212A*

The Mystery of Revelation
An intriguing account of a channeled conversation with Master Jesus fifty years after his crucifixion. *Item #7212B*

The Life and Times of John the Baptist
The awesome journey of the man who was the "Bridge between the Old and New Testament." *Item #7212C*

The Agendas of Peter and Paul
Many historical questions surrounding Peter "The Rock" and Paul "The Architect of Western Religion" are answered." *Item #7212D*

The Life and Times of Master Jesus
Kirael reveals many unknown facts of Jesus' journey and message of healing through love. *Item #7212E*

Conversations At the Last Supper
Kirael's astounding account of the conversations that took place among the 12 men and 12 women disciples the night before the crucifixion of Master Jesus. *Item #7212F*

HEALING CDs

The Power of Healing Prayers
By Rev. Fred Sterling

With a background of inspiring meditation music, Kirael, through the mediumship of Rev. Fred Sterling, creates prayers that guide you to heal and to change your life: *Start the Day, Release Fears, Heal the Physical Body, Balance and Center the Emotions, Understand the Children, Release Anger with Love, and Heal from the Loss of a Loved One*

"It's so beautifully put together! I learned how to pray from listening to this CD. You never get tired of listening to these prayers. It's a lifeline for me."—Clara Okazaki, Kailua, Hawaii

Item #7301A   *$15.95*

Emerald Breeze
by "El" Lopez

An enchantment of soft sounds produces a path for the mind to follow. Simply sit back and let go. This CD will create the space for you to clear the day's busy adventures. Let yourself drift into the solitude of the peaceful mind while "El" releases the true power of meditative sounds.

"When 'El' asked me to listen to these meditations in hopes that I would find a suitable title for the CD, little did I know how many times I would have to listen to complete the journey. As I tried to listen, I constantly fell into a deep meditative state. That is how good it is."   —"The Rev" Fred Sterling

Item #43EL01   *$12.95*

Awakening...To the Reality That You Are Never Alone
by Silke Vogelmann-Sine, Ph.D.

Dr. Silke, a licensed psychologist with over 20 years of experience helping people to heal, introduces a new and astonishing view into our relationships with the higher vibrations of the non-physical self, stirring the emotions to new levels by creating a special safe space where one can begin to experience deep-seated emotional healings.

"Healing is a gift that we all share. I would like to share these guided meditations with optional journaling exercises to help you experience and explore your own personal connection to your innermost self, and create a new life filled with limitless possibilities for health, peace, joy and love."—Silke Vogelmann-Sine, Ph.D.

Item #43SV01   *$15.95*

VIDEOTAPES

THE SHIFT TO YOUR HIGHER SELF
Learn about the Four Pillars of Conscious Creation and how you can use them in your life. The video covers *Prana-Breathing, Masterminding, Prayer, Meditation.* Narrated by Rev. Fred Sterling and Rev. Carol Morishige.
Length: 60 minutes VHS **ITEM #2401 $19.95**

THE MESSENGER VOLUMES I & II
An exclusive TV interview with Kirael from the Seventh Dimension. Interviewed by Rev. Carol Morishige, Kirael discusses the journey from fear to love and how to embrace with love the changes that the new millennium will bring.
Length: 60 minutes VHS **ITEM #7401 $19.95**

YOUR INFORMATION RESOURCE FOR THE GREAT SHIFT

I.D.	Product Title	Price
7101	**Book:** Kirael: The Great Shift by Rev. Fred Sterling	$14.95
7102	**Book:** Kirael Volume II: The Genesis Matrix by Rev Fred Sterling	$14.95
7161	**Book:** The Kirael Collection: Guide to the Unseen Self by Rev. Fred Sterling	$14.95
7161-01	**Downloadable Book:** The Kirael Collection: Guide to the Unseen Self	$9.95 at Kirael.com
7301A	**CD:** The Power of Healing Prayers, Volume I by Kirael	$15.95
7401	**Video:** Kirael: The Messenger–Vol. I & II–VHS Format	$19.95
2401	**Video:** The Shift to Your Higher Self–VHS Format	$19.95
2201	**Meditation Audiotape:** "Inward Quest" by Rev. Fred Sterling	$9.95
	90-minute Audiotapes by Kirael—in digital stereo:	
7299-01A	How to Have It All: The Ten Principles of Conscious Creation (10-Audiotape set)	$69.95
7200S	"An Evening with Kirael"—Audiotape subscription/one year	$100.00
7201	Angels	$9.95
7202	Aspects and Splinters	$9.95
7203	Christ Consciousness	$9.95
7204	The Female Energies that Surrounded Christ	$9.95
7205	The Galactic Brotherhood	$9.95
7206	The Great Shift	$9.95
7207	Photon Energy	$9.95
7208	Sharing Life With Your Ego	$9.95
7209	Signature Cell Healing	$9.95
7210	Time, Space—The Illusion	$9.95
7211	Transitioning Into the Light	$9.95
7212	Wisdom of the Lost Scrolls Series (6 audiotapes)	$47.95
7212A	The Book of Genesis	$9.95
7212B	The Book of Revelation	$9.95
7212C	The Life and Times of John the Baptist	$9.95
7212D	The Agendas of Peter and Paul	$9.95
7212E	The Life and Times of Master Jesus	$9.95
7212F	Conversations at the Last Supper	$9.95
7500S	Monthly "Kirael Shift Report" mailed newsletter subscription for 1 year	$24.00
7599	**Church Doctrine Booklet:** A Guidebook to Move from Fear to Love	$3.00
43EL01	**Meditation CD:** Emerald Breeze by El Lopez	$12.95
43SV01	**CD:** Awakening… To the Reality That You Are Never Alone by Dr. Silke Vogelmann-Sine	$15.95

**Call *1-800-390-1886* for further information on these products and new
products unfolding as we go to print, or email: *ShopKirael@Kirael.com*
Order on-line at *www.Kirael.com***

WWW.KIRAEL.COM

A home for seekers, dedicated to the truths of love and healing, a place to learn about the global shift in consciousness and how it affects you.

You will find a wealth of information and resources on a wide variety of topics, including:

- Monthly Kirael Shift Reports

- Photon energy forecasts

- On-line healing room

- Kirael's numerology

- Library of channeled articles

- Tools for the Shift, and much more...

"THE GREAT SHIFT WITH FRED STERLING"

Weekly Internet/Radio Broadcast

Connect to the program through *Kirael.com*

Listeners have the opportunity to call in and talk live with Fred Sterling and his special guests. In the second hour of the program, Rev. Sterling moves his consciousness aside and allows Kirael to bring his loving wisdom through.

What's new that everyone's talking about? Long-distance healing sessions taking place on the program! Tune in and send your energy.

Kirael.com is a grassroots, non-profit effort, designed and run by volunteers and part-time staff at the Honolulu Church of Light.

When you're in Hawai'i be sure to visit...

THE HONOLULU CHURCH OF LIGHT
A Healing Sanctuary

Led by Senior Minister and Director, *Reverend Fred Sterling*, the church was founded on the trinity of Truth, Trust and Passion to create a space whereby all religious understandings are welcomed.

Our programs and services include:

- Sunday and Wednesday evening healing services
- Free Signature Cell Healing sessions, available by appointment
- Spiritual counseling services
- Prayer Services and Meditation Evenings
- Personal, Business or Community Blessings/Healings
- "Evenings with Kirael" monthly live medium sessions

Is There a Wedding in Your Future?

The Honolulu Church of Light creates a loving and healing space where couples marrying for the first time, or seeking a new beginning in their marriage, may come to Lemuria to express their love for each other on new levels of commitment and spiritual fulfillment. Full-wedding packages are available at affordable rates. We specialize in spiritual wedding vow renewals.

Please call the church for more information

The Honolulu Church of Light

1-800-390-1886
www.Kirael.com Email: *theshift@Kirael.com*